THE

SAINTS' INHERITANCE.

THE

SAINTS' INHERITANCE

BY

J. N. LOUGHBOROUGH.

"Blessed are the meek, for they shall inherit the earth." Matt. v, 5.

STEAM PRESS OF THE REVIEW AND HERALD OFFICE.
BATTLE, CREEK, MICH.

1859.

Facsimile Reproduction

Copyright © 2005 TEACH Services, Inc.
ISBN-13: 978-1-57258-303-0
Library of Congress Control Number: 2004112330

Published by

TEACH Services, Inc.
www.TEACHServices.com

PREFACE.

Dear Reader : In the following pages we propose to occupy your attention for a time with some inquiries respecting the future inheritance that is to be received and enjoyed by those who live truly faithful to God. We here set up the claim that it is to be this earth redeemed from the curse, when the works of the Devil shall have been burned out of it, and when it shall stand forth as beautiful and glorious as when it came from the hands of its plastic Creator, who then pronounced it "*very good.*"

Although you may have supposed that the saints are to receive their recompense "Beyond the bounds of time and space," do not start back at the idea that they are to receive a literal kingdom, consisting of literal territory ; but carefully read the evidences which have brought us to the conclusion that it is to be the "kingdom, and dominion, and greatness of the kingdom under the whole heavens," which shall be finally given to the saints of God as their eternal abode.

As Dr, J. CUMMINGS, of England, says, " We have got a notion as if there were something essentially impure and hopeless in what is material, . , , But it is not so. Only exhaust from the earth the poison, sin—let the footfall of Him who made it be echoed from the hills and valleys once more, at dewy dawn, and at even tide, and this earth of ours will be instantly transformed into an orb, the like of which is not amid all the orbs of the universe besides.''

We have endeavored to show in these few pages that not only holy men of past ages, and the present age, have looked for a kingdom to be established on the earth redeemed from the curse, but that God's word plainly teaches that this earth shall become finally the saints' inheritance. Whatever may be your faith, or standing, grant us all that toleration you would claim for yourself; then read and ponder.

J. N, LOUGHBOROUGH.

Battle Creek, March, 1859.

SAINTS' INHERITANCE.

"Blessed are the meek; for they shall inherit the earth."
Matt. v, 5.

THE sentiment of the above text is not peculiar to the New Testament; but is also fully declared in the Old. In Ps. xxxvii, it is three times stated that the Lord's people shall inherit the *earth*," and three times that "they shall inherit the *land*." We understand that these texts declare a future inheritance. Not an inheritance of the blessings of this life, but of the joys of the earth made new. Says the reader, " I supposed Matt. v, 5, was fulfilled in this present life." But where is there a person that has received an inheritance here, because he has lived Christlike? (To be meek is to be like Christ.) Is not the decree still upon all men, "In the sweat of thy face shalt thou eat bread"? Are the righteous more favored with this world's goods than the wicked? Or does God still make the "sun to shine on the evil and on the good, and send rain on the just and on the unjust"?

We should judge from the manner in which David treats this subject, that he did not consider that the righteous now inherit the earth. Although he could say, "I have been young, and now am old, yet have I not seen the righteous forsaken, nor his seed begging bread;" yet when he speaks of abundant prosperity, he treats it as though it was the lot of the wicked, instead of the saints. Read

Ps. lxxiii. 3–7. I was envious at the foolish, when I saw the prosperity of the wicked." "For there are no bands in their death; but their strength is firm. They are not in trouble as other men." "Their eyes stand out with fatness; they have more than heart could wish." In Ps. xxxvii, 7, he says, "Fret not thyself because of him who prospereth in his way." But this is said of those who "bring wicked devices to pass."

The principal reason urged in support of the position that Matt. v, 5, applies in this life, is the supposition that when Christ comes to redeem his people, the earth will be destroyed, and man no longer possess it. If this position can be sustained, then, of course, all texts which speak of a reward, or punishment,- on this earth, must have their application before that time. Reasoning in accordance with this position, some have made capital of such texts as Prov. xi, 31. "The righteous shall be recompensed in the earth; much more the wicked and the sinner." Claiming that this text could not have its application after this life, they have reasoned that "whatever recompense is received by the righteous or wicked here, must be for their good or evil deeds performed here. And if the wicked have met the recompense of their evil deeds here, in another life they will have an equal chance with the righteous." But by comparing with this, two other proverbs of the wise man, we see that this fabric is without foundation. Prov. ii, 21, 22. "For the upright shall dwell in the land, and the perfect shall remain in it. But the wicked shall be cut off from the earth, and the transgressors shall be rooted out of it." Again, in Prov. x, 30, speaking of the righteous after they are planted in their inheritance, he says: "The righteous shall never be removed; but the wicked shall not inhabit the earth." Instead, then, of Prov. xi, 31 proving that all are recompensed in this life, we see it points to the final cutting off of the wicked. When the wicked are cut off, the "meek inherit the earth, and dwell therein forever."

As we have before stated, the principal reason urged why Matt. v, 5, applies in this life, is that the earth is not to exist after this probationary state shall have closed. If the above premise be true, that the earth is to be burned up at the second advent, and no more exist, then, of course, all texts speaking of an inheritance on earth, must be fulfilled before such a conflagration shall take place.

We know of but one text which has been pressed into the service of proving that the earth will cease to exist at the coming of Christ. It is 2 Pet. iii, 10, 12. "But the day of the Lord will come as a thief in the night, in the which the heavens shall pass away with a great noise, and the elements shall melt with fervent heat, the earth also, and the works that are therein shall be burned up." This text does not inform us that the earth is to be burned up; neither could such a conclusion be drawn from it after properly analyzing the language. It will be seen that to make sense, the word "also" must refer to what has been previously said; and instead of reading it—"The earth also and the works that are therein shall be burned up," it would read, "The elements shall melt with fervent heat, the earth also," showing that the earth is to be melted the same as "the elements." Next the Apostle notices the works in the earth, and tells us they shall be "burned up." So we perceive that it is the works which are in the earth, and not the earth itself, which are to be burned up in the day of the Lord. The works in the earth which are to be burned up, we understand are the "works of the Devil," which John says, Christ has been manifested that he might destroy." See 1 John iii, 8. These, we understand, are sin and sinners. The above conclusion, that the earth is to be melted instead of burned up, is confirmed by verse 11. "Seeing then that all these things shall be *dissolved*, what manner of persons ought ye to be in all holy conversation and godliness?" His claim here is not that the earth is be burned up, but *dissolved*. This is the only testimony we have met with to prove that the earth is to be burned up, and this makes no such statement. It is further evident that Peter did not design to teach the utter destruction of the heavens and the earth, from the fact that he immediately adds, "Nevertheless, we according to his promise, look for new heavens and a new earth, wherein dwelleth righteousness."

EDWARD ROBINSON, D. D., Professor at Andover says, that the original word, rendered *new*, in 2 Pet. iii, 13 ; Isa. lxv, 17, and lxvi, 22, means *renewed*, or *made new*, hence, better, superior, more splendid. So the corresponding word of the O. T., means, as a verb, to make new, or renew, repair, restore, as in 1 Sam. xi, 14 ; Job x, 17 ; Isa. lxi, 4 ; Ps. ciii, 5 ; 2 Chron, xv, 8 ; xxiv, 4 ; whence are derived the words rendered *new*, i. e., *renewed*, as in new moon, new heart, new creature, &c.

J. M. CAMPBELL, of England, meets objections on

this point as follows : " If you have difficulties as
to this matter I refer you to the 65th chapter of Isaiah. Read it, and see whether it is not manifest
that it is this very earth, in another state of it, that
is called the New Earth, and that it is in this very
earth where God has been dishonored, that God
is to be honored. I would further say to you, that
Satan may not take advantage of you, if any find
difficulties through the word *new*, that this word is
here used in some such way as when a converted
man is called 'a new creature.' I am the same
person as I was before conversion, yet am I a new
man ; so the earth will be the same globe of earth,
but still so changed as to be justly called a new
earth. Some ask, Do you think that Christ is to
come to this vile earth? Was it not enough that
he was once humbled? Shall he again leave glory for it ? He will not be on the earth as it now
is, but it shall be changed, and you are not to judge
of what this earth shall be when the curse is taken
off, and the power of God is put forth in beautify-
ing and glorifying it, by what it now is. You
might as well think to know what body a saint shall
have at the resurrection, by looking at the body he
now has. The saints shall dwell in bodies, but they
shall be glorified bodies ; and Christ shall reign on
earth, but it shall be the earth redeemed from the
curse."*

Allowing this criticism to be correct, there are no
grounds to claim from Peter that this earth is to be
annihilated. Solomon tells us, [Eccl. i, 4,] that
" the earth abideth forever."

*New Heavens and New Earth, by D. T. Taylor.

Reason would lead us to object to the idea that this earth is to be blotted out from the universe at the close of the probationary state. It will be freely admitted that since the early history of this earth, sin, rebellion, anarchy, and confusion, have distressed its borders; the mass of its inhabitants have lived in rebellion against the law of God, until, as John has expressed it, "We know that the whole world lieth in wickedness." We can expect nothing better in this probationary state; for Paul informs us that "evil men and seducers shall wax worse and worse, deceiving and being deceived." If there is no future state for this earth after sin and sinners are rooted out of it, it appears to us, its very existence would be a blot in the universe of God.

THE DUBLIN CHRISTIAN HERALD says : "If the earth was to be destroyed, and man never to have the sovereignty of it, Satan would have a victory to boast of forever; neither would that promise be fulfilled, that Jesus should destroy the works of the Devil. 1 John iii, 8. Frightful indeed is the breach which Satan has made in this fair field of God's creation; but Jesus is the repairer of the breach, . . . nor will he leave a single path unrestored to its original beauty. It is essential for Christ's glory that the earth should be delivered out of the hand of the enemy."*

THOMAS DICK, LL. D., says : "To suppose, as some have done, that the whole fabric of creation will be shattered to pieces, that the stars will literally fall from their orbs, and the material universe be blotted out of existence, is a sentiment so absurd and extrav-

* Ibid.

agant, and so contrary to the general tenor of scripture
and the character of God, that it is astonishing that
it should ever have been entertained by any man
calling himself a divine, or a Christian preacher.
I have already had occasion to remark, that there
is no example of annihilation, or an entire destruction of material substances, to be found in the universe. We have no reason to believe that even
those changes to which our world is destined at the
general conflagration, will issue in its entire destruction. The materials of which the earth and its atmosphere are composed will still continue to exist
after its present structure is deranged, and will, in
all probability, be employed in the arrangement of
a new system purified from the physical evils which
now exist, and which may continue to flourish a
monument of Divine power and wisdom through-
out an infinite lapse of ages."*

JOHN CUMMING, D. D., of London, says: "When
he (Christ) comes, this earth shall be re-cast, restored, re-constituted, re-beautified, and set in more
than its first and pristine glory. I never can bring
myself to believe that this beautiful earth, its beau-
ties still outnumbering its blemishes, is to be annihilated. I cannot bring myself to believe that the
Devil's success is to be crowned with victory at the
last day, and that this orb, which God made fair,
beautiful and holy, and which sin has made as it is,
and over which the old serpent has left his trail, so
long, so far, and so wide, he means to resign to Satan. But it is not a matter of conjecture. God
has positively stated that it shall be restored. We

* Philosophy of a future state, Part II, ¶ 17.

have got a notion as if there were something essentially impure and hopeless in what is material. We have the old gnostic heresy, that stone, tree, and flower, must be, by their very structure and organization, bad and impure. But it is not so. Only exhaust from the earth the poison, sin—let the footfall of Him who made it be echoed from its hills and valleys, once more, at dewy dawn, and at even tide, and this earth of ours will be instantly transformed into an orb, the like of which is not amid all the orbs of the universe besides."*

This leads us to inquire, What is the

PURPOSE OF GOD CONCERNING THE EARTH?

Without the light of revelation we can give no true answer to the above question. But if God has made known his purpose concerning the earth, we shall not be considered on forbidden ground in examining a few scripture testimonies on this subject. Was it the plan of God concerning the creation of this earth that it should remain in the hands of the wicked about six thousand years, and then be burned up? We have often heard people speak of what is to take place "amid the crush of worlds." Is this system of planets thus to be thrown in confusion and destroyed? What saith the scripture on this point?

We read in Isa. xlv, 18, "For thus saith the Lord that created the heavens; God himself that formed the earth and made it; he hath established it, he created it not in vain, he formed it to be inhabited." Here it is plainly stated what God's de-

* New Heavens and Earth.

sign was in creating the earth. "He formed it to be inhabited." But, say you, It has been inhabited. Yes, but mostly by a race of rebels. Can we suppose that God's purpose concerning the earth has been entirely carried out in the past, while man has possessed the earth? God's purpose was that the earth should "be inhabited."

But it has been claimed by some that the earth will be purified, and then left to new inhabitants. Says POLLOK:

"So burned the earth upon that dreadful day,
Yet not to full annihilation burned:
The essential particles of dust remained,
Purged by the final, sanctifying fires,
From all corruption; from all stain of sin,
Done there by man or devil, purified,
The essential particles remained, of which
God built the world again, renewed, improved,
With fertile vale, and wood of fertile bough;
And streams of milk and honey, flowing song;
And mountains cinctured with perpetual green;
In clime and season fruitful, as at first,
When Adam woke, unfallen, in paradise.
And God, from out the fount of native light,
A handful took of beams, and clad the sun
Again in glory; and sent forth the moon
To borrow thence her wonted rays, and lead
Her stars, the virgin daughters of the sky.
And God revived the winds, revived the tides;
And touching her from his Almighty hand,
With force centrifugal, she onward ran,
Coursing her wonted path, to stop no more.
Delightful scene of new inhabitants!
As thou, this morn, in passing hither, saw.

Thus done, the glorious Judge, turning to right,
With countenance of love unspeakable,
Beheld the righteous, and approved them thus.
'Ye blessed of my Father, come ye just,
Enter the joy eternal of your Lord;

Receive your crowns, ascend and sit with me,
At God's right hand, in glory evermore.' "
[Course of Time, B. x.

God gave the earth to man, [Gen. i, 26,] and
gave him "dominion over the fish of the sea, over
the fowl of the air, and over the cattle, and over *all
the earth*, and over every creeping thing that creepeth upon the earth." From this we should learn
that God designed that man, not some other race,
should inhabit the earth. With this agrees also the
language of David, when he says, [Ps. cxv, 16,]
"The heaven, even the heavens, are the Lord's;
but the earth hath he given to the children of men."
But when the earth was thus given to man, he was
in an upright state, and the Lord had pronounced
him, with the rest of his works, "very good." Solomon says, [Eccl. vii, 29,] "This only have I found,
that God made man upright; but they have sought
out many inventions." Seeing the manner in which
the Lord has dealt with man, we should conclude
his purpose was that man, in an upright state,
should possess the earth; for he was in an upright
state when God gave him dominion over the earth.
This probationary state while in the garden, or rather, the manner in which man rebelled and transgressed the word of the Lord, cut him off from the
further enjoyment of even the glorious place he
then possessed. When he became sinful, he lost
that dominion.

A skeptical mind might, perhaps, be ready to
claim here that God's purpose had been frustrated
in the fall of man. Although it may seem to them
that God's purpose has been frustrated, yet we believe, and shall endeavor to show, that God's pur-

pose will yet be carried out, and the earth will be possessed by man in an upright state. Says Peter, " We look for new heavens and a new earth, (*renewed earth*,) wherein dwelleth righteousness." Some paraphrase this, " Wherein the righteous shall dwell," which gives probably the correct idea. Then will God's purpose respecting the earth be fully accomplished.

David seemed to have his mind on such a glorous inheritance. While speaking of the final overthrow of the wicked, he contrasts with it a possession of the earth by the people of God. He says, [Ps. xxxvii, 1–3,] " Fret not thyself because of evil doers, neither be thou envious against the workers of iniquity. (The reason we would be liable to fret is plainly stated in verse 7 : ' Fret not thyself because of him who *prospereth* in his way.') For they shall soon be cut down like the grass, and wither as the green herb. Trust in the Lord and do good, so shalt thou dwell *in the land*, and verily thou shalt be fed." Some might claim that this text applies in this life; but being contrasted with the cutting off of the wicked, we must conclude that the " dwelling in the land" is after the wicked are cut off.

Again we read in verses 9–11, " For evil doers shall be be cut off; but those that wait on the Lord, they shall inherit the earth. For yet a little while, and the wicked shall not be; yea, thou shalt diligently consider his place, and it shall not be; but the meek shall inherit the earth, and shall delight themselves in the abundance of peace." Some have sought to apply this text to the present state ; but it seems that Job saw no chance for abundance

of peace here; but speaking of the grave he said,
"There the wicked *cease* from troubling, and the
weary be at rest." There will be a time of abundance of peace ; but it will be after the "wicked
shall not be." We cannot claim that the cutting
off of the wicked in this chapter is simply cutting
them off from this life; for he says in verse 20,
"But the wicked shall perish, and the enemies of
the Lord shall be as the fat of lambs; they shall
consume ; into smoke shall they consume away."

These testimonies of the Psalmist clearly speak
of a future inheritance of this earth, and, indeed,
many of those who have stood high as christians in
the past, have believed and advocated a future possession of this earth. Before passing directly to an
examination of this subject, we will present a few
testimonies under the head of,

FAITH OF GOOD MEN.*

Martin Luther, in his *Table Talk*, p. 322,
says: "God will make not the earth only, but the
heavens also, much more beautiful than they are at
present. At present we see the world in its working clothes, but hereafter it will be arrayed in its
Easter and Whitsuntide robes."

Calvin, on Isaiah xi, says: The Prophet "asserts
here the change of the nature of wild beasts, and
the restoration of the creation as at first."

Luther said: "God will come to judgment and
amend all things in this world." Again he says of
the earth and elements: "They will lose their former nature, and be endued with another."

---

*For most of the quotations under this heading we are
indebted to the work called New Heavens and New
Earth, by *D. T. Taylor*.

ARCHBISHOP CRANMER in his Catechism authorized by king Edward VI, taught that there would be "a renovation of all things." "So for man's sake for whose use the great world was created, being at length renovated, it shall put on a face that shall be far more pleasant and beautiful."

JOSEPH MEDE, of the seventeenth century, thus paraphrases 2 Pet iii, 13: "But this conflagration ended, we look according to his promise, [Isa. lxv, 17, and lxvi, 22,] for a new heaven and a new earth, that is, a new and refined state of the world, wherein righteousness shall dwell, according as the same Prophet saith, [Isa. lx, 20, 21,] Thy people also shall be all righteous, they shall inherit the land, or earth, forever."

DR. GOODWIN wrote: "God doth take the same world that was Adam's, and makes it new and glorious. The same creation groaneth for this new world, this new clothing—as we groan to be clothed upon, so doth this whole creation. Rom. viii, 19–23. And as God takes the same substance of man's nature, and engrafteth the new creature upon it, the same man still; so he takes the same world and makes it a new world to come for the second Adam. For the substance of the same world shall be restored to a glory which Adam could never have raised it unto. And this God will do before he hath done with it, and this restitution is 'the world to come.' Heb. ii, 5."

THE ENTIRE BODY OF BAPTISTS, in the time of Charles II, in their Confession of Faith say: "We believe that the new Jerusalem that shall come down from God out of heaven, when the tabernacle of God shall be with men, and he shall dwell with

2

them, will be the metropolitan city of his kingdom, and will be the glorious place of residence of
both Christ and his saints forever, and will be so
situated as that the kingly palace will be on Mount
Zion, the holy hill of David, where his throne was."

MILTON says:

"The world shall burn, and from her ashes spring
New heavens and earth wherein the just shall dwell,
And after all their tribulations long,
See golden days."

JOSHUA SPAULDING and COTTON MATHER affirm
that "The new heavens and the new earth was the
country promised to Abraham, and to his seed :
which neither he nor they received, but desired and
sought, having seen afar off."

PHILIP DODDRIDGE wrote: "We shall go from the
ruins of a dissolving world, to the new heavens and
new earth, wherein righteousness forever dwells."

GEORGE BENSON said: "We expect Christ's second advent to restore all things—to establish a
kingdom of righteousness upon earth—and to begin his glorious reign."

TOPLADY in his sermon on Rev. xxi, 5, affirms
that "a day will dawn when a period shall be put
to every disorder under which nature at present la-
bors, and the earth will become just what it was,
perhaps considerably better than it was, ere sin destroyed the harmony and broke the balance cf the
well-according system."

JOHN WESLEY says on the text "Behold I
make all things new." "The line of this prophecy
does not end with the present world, but shows us
the things that will come to pass when this world
is no more. For thus saith the Creator and Gov-

ernor of the universe, 'Behold I make all things new;' all which are included in that expression of the Apostle: ' A new heaven and a new earth,"*

Dr. Adam Clarke says: "The present earth, though destined to be burned up, will not be destroyed but be renewed, and refined, purged from all moral and natural imperfections, and made the endless abode of blessed spirits." †

Dr. Urwick of Dublin, on 2 Pet. iii says: " Another mundane sphere will arise out of the ruins of the present, forming a region of perfect sinlessness, to which the saved look forward as their abode." " Novel as the thought may be to some persons, the Lord, mighty in battle, who on the cross spoiled principalities and powers and made a show of them openly, and who age after age is breaking the yoke of the oppressor, and emancipat-- ing human souls, will not stay in his career of illustrious achievements till he wrest the very earth itself from the grasp of its usurper, re-creating it in unrivalled purity and glory, and taking possession of it with his people for immortality as peculiarly his own domain."

A. Thouluck D. D., an eminent German divine, says: "The glorification of the visible creation is more definitely declared in Rev. xxi, 1; although it must be borne in mind that a prophetic vision is there declared. Still more definitely do we find the belief of a transformation of the material world declared in 2 Pet. iii, 7–12. The idea that the perfected kingdom of Christ is to be transferred to heaven, is properly a modern notion. According to

*Sermon lxix, † Comments on 2 Pet. iii.

Paul and the Revelation, the kingdom of God is placed upon the earth, in so far as this itself has part in the universal transformation. This exposition has been adopted and defended by the most of the oldest commentators; for example: Chrysostom, Theodoret, Jerome, Augustine, Luther, Koppe, and others."

Dr. JOHN PYE SMITH, of England says: " I cannot but feel astonishment, that any serious and intelligent man should have his mind fettered with the common, I might call it the vulgar, notion of a proper destruction of the earth; and some seem to extend the notion to the whole solar system, and even the entire material universe; applying the idea of an extinction of being, a reducing to nothingness. I confess myself unable to find any evidence of it in nature, reason, or Scripture. We can discover nothing like destruction in the matter of the universe as subjected to our senses. Masses are disintegrated, forms are changed, compounds are decomposed, but not an atom is annihilated . . . We according to his promise, look for new heavens and a new earth, wherein dwelleth righteousness."

JOSEPH D'ARCY SIRR, of England says: " Unless the new heaven and new earth were identical with the orb we inhabit and its atmosphere, it could never be said there was *no more* sea; that it was *no more*, or *no longer* implies that it had been before."

EDWARD HITCHCOCK, D. D., President of Amherst College, on 2 Pet. iii says: " Now, the Apostle does not here in so many words, declare that the new heavens and earth will be the present world and its atmosphere purified and renovated by fire; but it is certainly a natural inference that such was his meaning. For if he intended some other remote and quite different place, why should he call it earth, and, especially, why should he surround it with atmosphere? The natural and most obvious meaning of the passage surely is, that the future residence of the righteous will be this present terraqueous globe, after its entire organic and coumbustible matter shall have been destroyed, and its whole mass reduced by heat to a liquid state, and then a new economy reared up on its surface, not adapted to sinful but to sinless beings; and, therefore, quite different from its present condition —probably more perfect, but still the same earth and surrounding heavens."

Thomas Chalmers, D. D., the late eminent Scottish theologian says of the earth: "By the convulsions of the last day, it may be shaken, and broken down from its present arrangements, and thrown into such fitful agitations as that the whole of its existing framework shall fall to pieces; and with a heat so fervent as to melt its most solid elements, it may be utterly dissolved. And thus may the earth again become 'without form and void,' [Jer. iv, 23,] but without one particle of its substance going into annihilation. Out of the ruins of this second chaos, may another heaven and another earth be made to arise, and a new materialism, with other aspects of magnificence and beauty, emerge from the wreck of this mighty transformation, and the world be peopled as before with the varieties of material loveliness, and space be again lighted up into a firmament of material splendor."

Alexander Pope, Bishop Heber, and Dr.

ISAAC WATTS have sung of this glorious time. Says WATTS:

"Yet when the sounds shall tear the skies
And lightnings burn the globe below,
Saints, you may lift your joyful eyes,
There's a new heaven and earth for you."

A host of others have endorsed the same view, among whom we might mention MATTHEW HENRY, MATTHEW POOLE, in his Annotations, RICHARD BAXTER, THOMAS BURNET in his Theory of the Earth, JOHN BUNYAN, INCREASE MATHER, THOMAS JAMES, ANDREW FULLER, JOHN COX of England, and the eloquent EDWARD IRVING, who asks in his Orations, "And cannot God create another world many times more fair, and cast over it a mantle of light many times more lovely, and wash it with purer dew than ever dropped from the eyelids of the morning?" "O what a thought, that the deluge of sin shall be baled out, that the long-covered hills and valleys of holiness shall again present themselves, that the slimy path of the old serpent shall be cleansed out of all nations, and the alloy of hell with fervent heat be burnt out of the elements of the solid globe, that the kingdom peopled with the redeemed shall become meet to be presented in the presence of God, and remain for ever."

SPECIAL PROMISES RESPECTING THE EARTH.

We have evidence which is conclusive to our mind that there is a future inheritance of this earth. This evidence we will present in the form of a logical argument. The first premise of this argument is: God has made certain infallible promises respecting this earth. Second. These promises have not

yet been accomplished, and according to the description the Bible gives of the last days they cannot meet their accomplishment this side of the second advent of Christ. After sustaining these premises we shall draw the fair and logical conclusion;
therefore there is a future for this earth beyond
the second advent when the saints of God shall
possess it, and these promises be fulfilled.

The first promise of this character we will notice
is Num. xiv, 21. "But as truly as I live, all the
earth shall be filled with the glory of the Lord."
There can be no doubt as to the certainty of the
fulfillment of this promise, for the Lord has pledged
his own life for its accomplishment. The history
of the past presents no testimony that the earth has
ever thus been filled with the Lord's glory, But in
every age since this prediction, violence, anarchy and
sin have reigned predominant. It seems in the
days of Habakkuk, prophetic seers were still point-
ed to that glorious time as yet future. We read
[Hab. ii, 14] "For the earth *shall be* filled with the
knowledge of the glory of the Lord, as the waters
cover the sea." To avoid the conclusion that this
refers to a perfect state, when "the people shall be
all righteous," some have suggested that " there are
islands in the sea which are not covered by the waters, so there may be people even in this glorious
time that are still rebellious." But to show that
this is not the prophet's meaning, we would refer
you again to the first promise. "ALL the earth shall
be filled with the glory of the Lord." And Jeremiah speaking of the glorious time in the future
for God's people [chap. xxxi, 34] says: " And they
shall teach no more every man his neighbor, and

every man his brother, saying Know the Lord: for they shall all know me from the least of them unto the greatest of them, saith the Lord: for I will forgive their iniquity, and I will remember their sin no more."

We claim concerning these promises that they will not be fulfilled this side the second advent of Christ. It has been commonly claimed however, that the world is to be converted and a thousand years of peace and quietness be enjoyed by God's people on earth prior to Christ's coming again, and, that during that thousand years these promises are to be fulfilled.

The general tenor of Scripture, especially those portions that describe the last days, cannot be harmonized with the view that there is to be a temporal millennium, or world's conversion before the second advent. The testimony of Christ, as also that of Paul, is clearly against the view of the world's conversion. We read [Matt. xiii,] concerning the tares of the field: "The servants said unto him, Wilt thou then that we go and gather them up? But he said, nay . . . let both grow together until the harvest; and in time of the harvest I will say to the reapers, gather ye together first the tares," &c. Now mark his language when the disciples had demanded an explanation of this parable. Verses 38–40. "The good seed are the children of the kingdom; but the tares are the children of the wicked one . . . the harvest is the end of the world. . . As therefore the tares are gathered and burned in the fire: so shall it be in the end of this world." From this we see that both righteous and wicked are to be together on earth till the end of the world. So the world will not be converted prior to the second advent.

Paul, speaking of the state of the world just prior to the second advent, says [2 Tim. iii, 1–5] "This know also, that in the *last* days perilous times shall come; for men shall be lovers of their own selves, covetous, boasters, proud, blasphemers, disobedient to parents, unthankful, unholy, without natural affection, trucebreakers, false accusers, incontinent, fierce, despisers of those that are good, traitors, heady, highminded, lovers of pleasures more than lovers of God : having a form of godliness but denying the power thereof: from such turn away." It seems from the above language that a very degenerate mass of nominal professors are to exist in the very time where it is claimed that the world will enjoy a millennium. There can be no days later than the last, so " the last days" must include the very *last* day; therefore the above is a description of the state of a class just before the end of probation. In verse 8 Paul says of them, " As Jannes and Jambres withstood Moses, so do these also resist the truth." It cannot be that "*all* the earth" is filled with the glory of the Lord while such a class are still upon it.

Again Paul speaks of the last days [1 Tim. iv, 1] " Now the Spirit speaketh expressly that in the *latter times* some shall depart from the faith, giving heed to seducing spirits and doctrines of devils." Then instead of the church exerting her influence to such an extent as to convert the world, many will throw off restraint and " depart from the faith." The doctrine of devils will be taught by seducing spirits, and many will give heed to them. This we understand is already being accomplished in the teaching and progress of modern Spiritualism. We might mention Leroy Sunderland, and scores of others who have once been teachers of God's word, who have now denounced the Bible as priest-craft, and are fully given up to the spirits. This state of things above described, which we see rapidly drawing on, does not look like a triumph of the gospel in the last days, or a binding of Satan prior to Christ's second advent.

But says DR. PRIEST and others, "Christ is coming spiritually, Satan is to be bound, and a thousand years of millennium be enjoyed by God's people on the earth prior to Christ's coming to judgment." We reply. The word of God tells of no spiritual coming of Christ. His testimony to his disciples, when giving them their commission to preach the gospel, was, [Matt. xxviii, 19, 20,] "Go ye therefore and teach all nations, baptizing them in the name of the Father, and of the Son, and of the Holy Ghost . . . and lo, I am with you alway, even to the end of the world." Of course, we understand he promises in this testimony that his Spirit shall abide with them, even as we read concerning the Comforter which he promised to send. John xiv, 16. "And I will pray the Father, and he shall give you another Comforter, that he may abide with you for ever." So it would be folly to talk of a spiritual advent of Christ before the end of the world, unless it could first be shown that the above promises had failed, and his Spirit had left the world.

We know of no testimony which represents that Christ is yet to come spiritually. His coming will be real. When he had given to the disciples their

commission to preach the gospel, he ascended up
before them literally, and bodily, into heaven. See
Acts i, 10, 11. "And while they looked steadfast-
ly toward heaven as he went up, behold, two men
stood by them in white apparel which also said,
Ye men of Galilee, why stand ye gazing up into
heaven? this *same* Jesus which is taken up from
you into heaven, shall so come in like manner as ye
have seen him go into heaven." Jesus' coming is to
be as literal and visible as his ascension into heaven.
There is then no grounds to claim that the promise
that "the earth shall be filled with the glory of
the Lord" can be fulfilled this side the literal coming of our Lord from heaven. On the promises we
have thus far noticed respecting the earth, we have
sustained our two premises, and now respecting
them draw our logical conclusion. Therefore there
must be a future state for this earth beyond the second advent, when the "glory of God shall fill the
earth as the waters cover the sea."

Do any still further urge the idea of a millennium
prior to Christ's coming? we would say, if you locate a millennium this side his coming, it will be
strongly infected with the Papacy. We read of the
"little horn," (Papacy,) Dan. vii, 21, 22. "I beheld, and the same horn made war with the saints,
and prevailed against them, until the Ancient of
days came, and judgment was given to the saints of
the Most High; and the time came that the saints
possessed the kingdom." Again, Paul speaking of
this power, [2 Thess. ii,] calls it "that man of sin,
the son of perdition, who opposeth and exalteth
himself above all that is called God, or that is wor-
shipped." He says of him [verse 8,] "Whom the

Lord shall consume with the spirit of his mouth, and destroy by the brightness of his coming. So we clearly see the Papal power is to exist, even down to the point when Christ "shall be revealed from heaven with his mighty angels in flaming fire taking vengeance on them that know not God and obey not the gospel," &c.

But we now wish to call attention to another promise which the Lord has made respecting the earth. It is

THE PROMISE MADE TO ABRAHAM.

Some are ready to object to our dwelling on the promise made to Abraham, and wish us to confine ourselves to the teachings of the gospel. Well, if we were to acquiesce in their request and preach the gospel, (which we hope we shall ever be found doing) we must needs teach elementary principles before entering upon the great truths of the gospel. Those first principles must be connected with the first gospel sermons, and therefore some of these must be connected with this promise, for Paul says, [Gal. iii, 8,] God "preached before the gospel unto Abraham." The gospel as proclaimed at the very commencement of the present age declared the approach of a kingdom. Said John, [Matt. iii, 2.] "Repent, for the kingdom of heaven is at hand." A kingdom consists of territory and a king, as well as laws and subjects. This promise to Abraham we understand has reference to the territory and king. And so in examining this promise we shall not be departing from the commission to preach Christ's gospel.

We will now notice this promise, recorded Gen.

xiii, 14, 15. "And the Lord said unto Abraham, after that Lot was separated from him, Lift up now thine eyes, and look from the place where thou art, northward, and southward, and eastward, and westward; For *all the land* which *thou* seest, *to thee* will I give it, and to thy seed for ever."

After the Lord made this covenant with Abraham and was about to confirm it, he said to him, [chap. xv, 13–15,] "Know of a surety that thy seed shall be a stranger in a land that is not theirs, and shall serve them; and they shall afflict them four hundred years; and also that nation whom they shall serve, will I judge: and afterward shall they come out with great substance. And *thou* shalt go to thy fathers in peace; *thou* shalt be buried in a good old age."

We are told by some, that these promises which were made to Abraham were concerning the temporal possession of the land of Canaan. To this we object.

1. If it was a temporal possession of the land that was promised, then Abraham would have received it in his life time; but according to Stephen's testimony, [Acts, vii, 5,] he never received it. "And he gave him none inheritance in it, no, not so much as to set his foot on." Therefore the inheritance promised was not a temporal possession of the land.

2. It could not be a temporal possession that was promised, for he was to have it for ever, and for an "*everlasting* possession." If we should admit that the terms for ever and everlasting are limited * in

---

* It is a point which cannot be disputed. that the terms *for ever* and *everlasting* are sometimes limited in their meaning. Greenfield defines the original terms which

this testimony, and the promise had been fulfilled, we should find Abraham still on the land; * for the land still exists.

In Gen. xvii, 1–8 the Lord enters into covenant with Abraham respecting the possession of the land. Certain conditions are given to Abraham by which he and his seed are to receive the blessings of the covenant, the possession of the land.

"And when Abram was ninety years old and nine, the Lord appeared to Abram, and said unto him, I am the Almighty God; walk before me, and *be thou perfect*, and I will make my covenant between me and thee." This charge given to Abraham, as we learn by the marginal reading of the text, was to "be upright, or sincere." Uprightness and sincerity can only be developed by a perfect law, and so we conclude that the very conditions here given by which the inheritance is to be obtained is keeping the law of God † The blessing

are translated *for ever* and *everlasting*: "Duration, finite or infinite: unlimited duration, eternity: a period of duration, past or future, time, age, lifetime, &c." Of the terms thus translated Dr. Clarke says that they signify "As long as the thing, considering the surrounding circumstances, can exist."

* If Abraham was to have the land for an everlasting possession, then he must hold the possession as long as the land continues. The everlasting is not limited by Abraham's life; but it is the possession which is to be everlasting.

† What this everlasting covenant was, the keeping of which would secure Abraham and his posterity an everlasting possession, we may further learn by reading 1 Chron. xvi, 15–17, in connection with other texts. "Be ye mindful always of *his covenant; the word which he commanded* to a thousand generations. Even of *the covenant*

of the covenant is stated again in verse 8: "And I will give unto thee, and to thy seed after thee, the land wherein thou art a stranger, all the land of Canaan, for an *everlasting* possession."

The promise made to Abraham was renewed to Isaac. Gen. xxvi, 1–5. The Lord said to him: "Sojourn in this land, and I will be with thee, and I will bless thee . . . and will give unto thy seed all these countries: and in thy seed shall all the nations of the earth be blessed. Because that Abraham obeyed my voice, and kept my charge, my commandments, my statutes, and my laws."

This promise we find also confirmed to Jacob, as he had a view of the ladder: Gen. xxviii, 13. "And behold the Lord stood above it, and said, I am the Lord God of Abraham thy father, and the God of Isaac: the land whereon thou liest, to thee will I give it, and to thy seed."

But we wish to trace the subject of the promise to Abraham still farther, and shall inquire

WHAT WAS THE NATURE OF THE ABRAHAM-
IC PROMISE?

Was this simply a promise that Abraham should have a temporal possession of the land of Canaan? If it was, the promise failed; for he died, as the Lord said he should, "in a good old age," and, as Stephen says, [Acts vii, 5,] "he gave him none in-

which he made with Abraham, and of his oath unto Isaac; and hath confirmed the same to Jacob, for a law, and to Israel for an everlasting covenant." Here the same covenant is mentioned that God made with Araham. He says it is " *The word which he commanded.*" By reading Deut. iv, 13, and v, 22, we learn that the word commanded was the ten commandments.

heritance in it, no not so much as to set his foot
on." We shall not admit that he did not receive it
because God has failed to fulfill on his part; but
shall claim that the promise of a possession made to
him is yet to be fulfilled, and will be fully realized
in a future possession of the earth. While it is
claimed by some that this promise to Abraham was
a temporal possession of the land, Paul says [Heb.
xi, 9;] "He sojourned in the land of promise as in
a strange country." It is vain that men strive to
find a fulfillment of this promise, either to Abraham
or his posterity in the past; for it cannot be done.
Simply a possession of the land of Canaan does not
meet the promise; for Paul says the promise was
that "he should be the *heir of the world.*" Rom.
iv, 13.

To gain further light concerning the nature of
the Abrahamic promise, we will look at the comments of Paul in Gal. iii, 16. " Now to Abraham
and his *seed* were the promises made. He saith
not, and to seeds * as of many: but as of one, and
to thy seed, which is Christ."

If the *seed* to whom the promise was made was
Christ, then the promise could not be fulfilled prior
to the coming of that seed, consequently, not *prior*
to the first advent of Christ. With the view above,
we readily perceive that there is no ground for the

* We cannot read Gal. iii, 16, without thinking (and
we may as well pen our thoughts here) how important
in reading the Bible, to read carefully. In this text before us, Paul has based his whole argument on the absence
of a single letter. If it had not been that the letter *s* was
not attached to the word "*seed,*" how different would
have been his conclusions; but the word having the sin-
gular instead of the plural form, Paul reasons as above.

claim which is made by some, that the promise made to Abraham was all fulfilled when the children of Israel sojourned in the land of Canaan. Were Abraham, Isaac, or Jacob with them when they went in to possess the land? No. "They carried up Joseph's bones." Here are four generations that did not receive the land while alive, and yet the Lord said to Abraham, " I will give it (the land) to thee." To Isaac he said, "For unto thee I will give all these countries." To Jacob he said, "The land whereon thou liest, to *thee* will I give it." See Gen. xvii, 1–8; xxvi, 4; xxviii, 13. If we allow any force to the above language, when this promise is fulfilled, Abraham, Isaac and Jacob will receive the promise, with the rest of God's people.

Although Christ is the seed to whom the promise was made, to the church has been granted the privilege of joint-heirship. Paul says, [Gal. iii, 29,] "If ye be Christ's, then are ye Abraham's seed, and heirs according to the promise." This text shows that the fulfillment of the Abrahamic promise is yet future; for Christ's children could not be said to be *heirs* of a promise that is fulfilled. This testimony from Gal. iii, shows (contrary to the faith of some) that the Jews after the flesh are not heirs simply because they are descendants of Abraham; but, as expressed in verse 9: "So then they which be of faith are blessed with faithful Abraham,"

Paul's testimony [Heb. xi,] shows this promise is yet to be fulfilled. Verses 8–10, "By faith Abraham, when he was called to go out into a place which he should *after* receive for an inheritance, obeyed; and he went out not knowing whither he went. By faith he sojourned in the land of prom-

3

ise, as in *a strange country*, dwelling in tabernacles with Isaac and Jacob, the heirs with him of the same promise; for he looked for a city which hath foundations, whose builder and maker is God." This testimony shows that when Abraham was in the land, the promise was not fulfilled; but "he should after" receive it. Again, when he receives the accomplishment of this promise he is to receive "a city whose builder and maker is God."

In verse 13, Paul testifies of these ancient worthies: "These all died in faith not having received the promises, but having seen them afar off, and were persuaded of them, and embraced them, and confessed that they were *strangers* and *pilgrims* on the earth." Paul can mean only one of two things in this statement: either that these worthies died and God never made any promise to them, or else they died without receiving the accomplishment of those promises which he had made. The latter, of course, is the only conclusion we can draw from the text. "Well," says the objector, "this means they died without seeing the Saviour; the promise is respecting him." True, the promise is respecting the Saviour; he is the true seed, and he is the one with whom we are to be *joint-heirs* to the land. And your admission proves too much for you; for the possession could not be till after the heir came.

Paul in this chapter mentions a number of worthies, and says time would fail to tell of them and the work they accomplished through faith. In verses 39, 40, he draws his conclusion in regard to them as follows: "And these all having obtained a good report through faith, received not the promise; God having provided some *better thing* for us,

that *they* without us should not be made perfect."
Some would fain draw their conclusion from this
text that God did not fulfill his promise to Abraham, because he had concluded to do better for his
people than he promised to Abraham. But we do
not so understand the text. The "better thing" is not
a better inheritance, but something better than that
these ancient worthies should receive the promise in
their day; which " better thing" is " that they without us should not be made perfect." It seems from
this text that this promise is yet future, and is to
be realized when all those whom Paul styles *us* shall
be gathered out by the gospel preaching. Paul
seems to locate the fulfillment of this promise in
the perfect state. Had this promise been accomplished to the ancient worthies, they would have
been " made perfect" " without us." It is to be accomplished when our perfection shall come, which
Paul clearly shows, [1 Cor. xiii,] is when " we shall
know even as we are known;" that is, when faith
is lost in sight—after Jesus comes.

We next inquire, How did Paul view himself in
connection with that promise? We read, [Acts
xxvi, 6–8,] " And now I stand and am judged for the
hope of the promise made of God unto our fathers;
unto which promise our twelve tribes, instantly
serving God day and night, hope to come. For
which hope's sake, king Agrippa, I am accused of
the Jews. Why should it be thought a thing incredible with you, that God should raise the dead ?"
Paul here represents himself as willing to be judged for his hope relative to the promise to the fathers. He saw at once that the people would inquire how Abraham, Isaac and Jacob could receive

this promise, as they were dead; for the promise was unto them, and therefore he inquires why they should think the resurrection incredible. It would be strange indeed if the apostle Paul should submit himself to be judged in a Roman court, liable to be condemned, because of a hope inspired by a promise that was all fulfilled. Paul's reasoning on this text shows clearly that the fulfillment of this promise is beyond the resurrection.

The Apostle's teaching, [Eph. i, 13, 14,] clearly shows that this earth is the place where God's people are to receive their full reward. He says, " Ye were sealed with that Holy Spirit of promise, which is the earnest of our inheritance until the redemption of

"THE PURCHASED POSSESSION."

In the text above quoted there is a possession spoken of which has been purchased, and is also to be redeemed. What is this possession that is to be redeemed? Heaven, says one. If it is heaven, then heaven has passed from the hands of the original possessor, or else it could not be redeemed. To take this view would also oblige us to claim that heaven had been purchased; for it is the purchased possession that is to be redeemed.

What possession has passed out of the hands of its original possessor? I answer, The earth. "The heaven, even the heavens, are the Lord's; but the earth hath he given to the children of men." The earth was given to man; but he has lost the dominion God gave him. Where is it? We shall claim that when he was tempted, and overcome by the Devil, he was brought in bondage to him. "Of

whom a man is overcome, of the same is he brought
in bondage;" [2. Pet. ii, 19.] and he would of course
claim the property of man until *his* lease runs out.
Therefore the Devil is represented in the New Testament scriptures, as the god of this world. Not
that he is the rightful possessor of the earth, but
by intrigue the Devil has usurped the dominion
which was given to man.

With this view of the subject we may understand
the testimony of Luke iv. The Devil said to Christ,
when he " showed him all the kingdoms of the
world," " That is delivered unto me, and to whom-
soever I will I give it." But, say you, this is only
the testimony of the Devil. Although it is his testimony, it may for all that be truth, and it furnishes
a solution to Luke iv, which otherwise remains
without an explanation. It is stated that the
Devil tempted Christ. It surely would be no temptation for him to offer to Christ that which was already Christ's, or to offer that which he himself did
not possess. But admitting that the Devil had
usurped man's dominion, and that he held, as he
claimed, " the kingdoms of this world and the glory
of them," and then the presentation of them by him
to Christ can be looked upon as a temptation.

This dominion which Satan had usurped was
promised, to be given to Christ. " Thou, O tower
of the flock, the strong hold of the daughter of
Zion, unto thee shall it come, even the *first dominion.*" Micah iv, 8. The first dominion was dominion over the earth, which man lost when he
yielded to the Devil. This dominion was to come
to Christ. But the manner in which he was to obtain it was to spill his blood, and by the suffering of

death obtain power to dethrone the usurper. The
Devil offered him one of the very objects which was
to be obtained by his death, and it was a temptation.
By an ignominious death upon the cross, Christ
was to obtain the first dominion. But, said the
Devil, you need not die to get the kingdom; "fall
down and worship me, and I will give it you."
That was a temptation. We will now notice

ISRAEL'S SOJOURN IN THE LAND.

While some contend that the promise to Abraham was fulfilled when the children of Israel sojourned in the land of Canaan, we contend that
they had only a temporal possession of the land,
which was typical of the final possession of the
earth. When they corrupted themselves with their
idols, and sinned against the Lord, their enemies
prevailed against them, overran their land, and dis-
possessed them of their cities. Temporal judgments
were thus brought upon them. All this we understand was to show them the necessity of obey-
ing God if they would have his favor. If any
would really be Abraham's children, according to
Christ's rule, they must "do the works of Abraham."

While the yearly services of the sanctuary were
kept up and strictly carried out, Israel would have
a yearly purging of rebels. Every one who, in the
day of atonement, would afflict his soul, would find
mercy; but those who would not do it must die.
It is strange to us how individuals with these
facts before their minds can claim that there are
any peculiar national blessings yet to be given to
the Jews after the flesh.

But we are digressing. This possession of the land of Canaan by the natural descendants of Abraham, we understand, as we before claimed, was a *type* of the possession promised to God's people. Therefore we can see a propriety in purging the profane from among the children of Israel, that they might be kept a holy seed, and thus their possession of the land typify that inheritance which none but righteous ones can enjoy.

When we come to the time of Zedekiah, the children of Israel had so corrupted themselves by disobeying the Lord's commandments, that the scepter was taken from them, and passed into the hands of the wicked kings of the earth. The testimony of the Lord to Zedekiah, just before he was carried captive to Babylon, was: "And thou, profane wicked prince of Israel, whose day is come when iniquity shall have an end, thus saith the Lord God, Remove the diadem, and take off the crown; this shall not be the same; exalt him that is low, and abase him that is high. I will *overturn, overturn, overturn it;* and it shall be no more till he come whose right it is, and I will give it him." Eze. xxi, 25–27.

The One, " whose right it is," is Christ. He is the seed "to whom the promise was made." In the above text we learn that after the scepter passed from God's people, it was to be three times overturned before it passed into the hand of him "whose right it is." When Zedekiah the high prince was "abased," the low prince of Babylon was exalted to rule over God's people. When the kingdom of Babylon was conquered by the Medes and Persians, and Israel became tributary unto them, the scepter was overturned once. Again, when the Medes and Persians were conquered by Alexander, and the Grecian kingdom established, the Lord's word was fulfilled, and "it," (the scepter, &c.,) was overturned the second time. And when, 31 years B. C., the celebrated battle of Actium brought Rome to her position of "mistress of the world," the scepter had been three times overturned. And so far as the prediction made against Zedekiah is concerned, he whose right it was might come and take possession of the kingdom.

THE DISCIPLES LOOKED FOR JESUS TO ESTABLISH A LITERAL KINGDOM.

When our Saviour commenced his teaching, the Jews were expecting the Messiah, not, however, in the form in which he came; but as a king to take to himself the scepter of the kingdom, and reign over Israel, and destroy his enemies. We see from the movements of the disciples of our Lord, that their minds were strongly impressed with the same idea; namely, that Christ was then to take possession of his kingdom. With this view of the subject we can understand the meaning of their words, when they said, " If thou art the king of the Jews, tell the people plainly." And at another time when Jesus had performed a notable miracle, he " perceived that they would come and take him by force to make him a king, and he departed into the mountains." John vi, 15. Again, when Christ rode up to Jerusalem seated upon a colt, what a shout of " hosannah to the son of David" was raised by the people. What caused them thus to shout? Did they understand that in a few hours he was to hang upon the rugged cross, and expire, while all nature should be convulsed? No, they supposed he was riding to Jerusalem to take possession of the kingdom and throne of his father David. But Jesus died. Sadness filled the hearts of his disciples, and when on the morning of the resurrection he appeared to the women of their company, it was "as they mourned and wept."

Why this mourning if they understood the plan of God for the salvation of lost man? Why such sadness if they really had faith in Jesus' resurrection? Why were they not looking forward with joyous hope to the third day when they should again see him whom their souls loved? Instead of their manifesting such feelings as we should expect them to have if they understood what was to be accomplished by the death of Christ, we behold two of them conversing sadly of their disappointment as they walked in the way to Emmaus. We read that Jesus drew near and walked with them, "and said unto them, What manner of communications are these that ye have one to another, as ye walk, and are sad?" They answered, " Art thou only a stranger in Jerusalem, and knowest not the things that are come to pass?" He said, " What things?" They said concerning Jesus of Nazareth: " the chief priests and our rulers delivered him to be condemned to death, and have crucified him. But we trusted that it had been he which should have *redeemed Israel;* and besides all this, to-day is the third day since these things were done. Yea, and certain women also of our company made us *astonished,* which were early at the sepulchre; and when they found not his body, they came, saying that they had seen

a vision of angels, which said that he was alive."
"Astonished" to hear of the resurrection of Christ?
Who would claim, with such testimony before them,
that they understood the plan of redemption, to be
accomplished through his death and intercession?
If they understood it, what necessity for Jesus to
begin "at Moses and all the prophets," and expound
"unto them in all the Scriptures the things concerning himself"? Their testimony then in this
conversation, that they trusted Christ would *redeem*
Israel, must, and does to our mind, embody the
idea that they supposed Christ would redeem them
from under the hand of the Romans, by whose
Tetrarchs they were then ruled in their civil affairs.
If Christ redeemed them from this, it would simply
be by establishing his kingdom.

This company returned to Jerusalem, however,
believers in Christ's resurrection, and with their
minds enlightened on the subject of Christ's death.
But did they banish from their minds the idea
that Christ was *then* to commence his reign? We
will see. In Acts i, 6 we read: "When they
therefore were come together, they asked of him,
saying, Lord, wilt thou at this time *restore* again
the kingdom to Israel?" They were now more
than ever satisfied that Christ was the one whose
right the kingdom was. He had been raised from the
dead, and himself had shown them that it was necessary that this should take place that the Psalms &c.
might be fulfilled. And now seeing nothing in the
way of its establishment, they asked the above
question respecting the kingdom: "Wilt thou at this
time *restore*" it. Israel once had it, but lost it in
the days of Zedekiah. The question is, will Christ

now restore it? They had not yet seemed to get the force of the parable which Jesus spake when he was nigh to Jerusalem, for the benefit of those who thought the kingdom of God was immediately to appear [Luke xix, 11, 12,] in which he showed that the Son of man (like the nobleman) must "go into a far country and return" before the kingdom could be established. The light also seemed to be obscured from their minds, which Christ gave them when their hearts were saddened on account of his telling them, "I go to him that sent me." "Whither I go ye cannot come." Said he, "I go to prepare a place for you. And if I go and prepare a place for you, I will *come again* and receive you to myself." John xiii, 33; xiv, 1–3. But we ask, What is his reply to their question concerning the restoration of the kingdom? Does he tell them that he will never restore it? "It is not for you to know the times or the seasons which the Father hath put in his own power." This is virtually admitting that the kingdom was to be restored to Israel: not after the flesh; but as Paul says, [Rom. ix, 8,] "The children of the promise are counted for the seed." "But," he says, "ye shall receive power, after that the Holy Ghost is come upon you: and ye shall be witnesses unto me both in Jerusalem, and in all Judea, and in Samaria, and unto the uttermost part of the earth." This seems to indicate that they would understand this matter, after they should receive the Holy Ghost and be endowed with power from on high. Christ had told them [John xvi, 13,] "When he, the Spirit of truth, is come, he will guide you into all truth: for he shall not speak of himself; but whatsoever he shall hear, that shall he speak;

aud he will shew you things to come." Peter was
among those who received this power, and has
borne testimony concerning the matter. His testimony will lead us to notice

THE TIME FOR THE ESTABLISHMENT OF THE KINGDOM.

It cannot be expected in this brief work, that we
can say much on this point. We shall however notice
few texts that have a bearing on this subject, and
for a more detailed exposition shall refer the reader
to works on the prophecies of Daniel, and the exposition of Matt. xxiv, published at the REVIEW
OFFICE, Battle Creek, Michigan. In selecting testimony on this point, we shall look at the texts
that speak of the bringing in of the new-earth state.
  Peter in his second epistle, [chap. iii, 10,] says:
" The day of the Lord will come as a thief in the
night; in the which the heavens shall pass away
with a great noise, and the elements shall melt
with fervent heat, the earth also, and the works
that are therein shall be burned up." Verse 13.
" Nevertheless we, according to his promise, look for
new heavens and a new earth, wherein dwelleth
righteousness." This testimony shows that the time
when the earth becomes an abode for righteousness,
or as some render the text, " wherein the righteous
shall dwell," is after the fires of the day of the Lord
have purged the works of the Devil out of it. This
must locate this inheritance after the destruction of
the wicked; for the prophet says: [Isa. xiii, 9;]
" Behold, the day of the Lord cometh, cruel both with
wrath and fierce anger, to lay the land desolate:
and he shall destroy the sinners thereof out of it."

Then the establishment of the kingdom on earth, must be after the second coming of Christ, and after the destruction of those " that know not God and obey not the gospel of our Lord Jesus Christ."

This kingdom follows those represented by the four beasts of Dan. vii. In verses 17, 18, we read " These great beasts, which are four, are four kings, which shall arise out of the earth. But the saints of the Most High shall take the kingdom, and possess the kingdom for ever, even forever and ever." The powers represented by the symbols of the four beasts are not complete until the little horn has accomplished its work. The kingdom is not given into the hands of the saints until the work of this little horn is completed; for by reading Daniel ii, where are introduced symbols of the same kingdoms, we learn that when the God of heaven sets up a kingdom, it is by the image's being dashed in pieces and becoming as the chaff of the summer's threshing floor," &c. But by comparing the work of the little horn, [Dan. vii,] with that of the "man of sin," [2 Thess. ii,] it will be clearly seen that they are identical, and therefore, that the work marked out as the stone's smiting the image on the feet can be nothing else than the events by which the nations are dashed in pieces at the coming of Christ. With these points before us, it must be clearly seen that the kingdom cannot be established prior to Christ's second advent.

The above conclusion is also confirmed by the testimony of Dan. vii, 21, 22: " I beheld, and the same horn made war with the saints, and prevailed against them; until the Ancient of days came, and judgment was given to the saints of the Most High;

and the time came that the saints possessed the kingdom." This shows that the time when the saints possess the kingdom is after judgment is given to the
saints. Verse 27 shows that our conclusion, previously made, concerning the locality of the kingdom, is correct. "And the kingdom and dominion, and the greatness of the kingdom *under the
whole heaven* shall be given to the people of
the saints of the Most High, whose kingdom is an
everlasting kingdom" &c. A kingdom under the
whole heaven could be nothing less than the whole
earth. This conclusion is also confirmed by the testimony of verse 18 : " But the saints of the Most
High shall *take* the kingdom," clearly implying that
they will take the same territory as their kingdom,
over which the four beasts have ruled.

But you have probably been ready to claim long
ere this, that the kingdom of God is spiritual, and
that it was established at the time of our Saviour's
first advent, because Christ said, as recorded in
Luke xvii, 20, 21 : " The kingdom of God is *within* you." This, it is claimed, is sufficient to show
that the kingdom is spiritual, as it was then said
to be *in* the disciples of Jesus. But are you sure
that the kingdom was *in* the disciples? We will
quote the testimony : " And when he was demanded of the *Pharisees,* when the kingdom of God
should come," &c. You see it was the Pharisees,
whom he had previously called hypocrites, to whom
he says " the kingdom of God is *within* you." Was
this spiritual kingdom established in the hearts of
hypocrites? It was, if Christ meant to teach them
by this testimony that the kingdom of God was in
their hearts. But, say you, the kingdom *is* in the

hearts of the saints, This text will not prove it.
The thing demanded in this text is, when shall the
kingdom of God come? Christ does not say as
some would claim, that it had already come, but
this very answer shows that the coming of the kingdom was a future event. He says "neither *shall*
they say (when it comes) Lo here!" &c.
    If Christ meant to teach in this text that the
kingdom had already come, what can you make of
the prayer he taught his people to pray, [Matt. vi,
10,] "Thy kingdom come"? Every saint to the end
of this age may pray, " *Thy kingdom come;*" because the kingdom will not come till the "nobleman" returns, "having received the kingdom."
The idea we gain from Luke xvii, 20, 21, is that
when the kingdom of God comes, it will not be in
a secret manner, but all will know it, and there will
be no opportunity or necessity for any to say, "Lo
here! or lo there!" for the kingdom of God will
be "within you." or, as the margin reads, "*among
you.*" That this is the idea Christ meant to teach,
is plain from what he immediately told his disciples. Verses 22–24. "And he said unto the disciples, The days will come, when ye shall desire to
see one of the days of the Son of man, and ye shall
not see it. And they shall say unto you, See here!
or, see there! go not after them, nor follow them;
for as the lightning, that lighteneth out of the one
part under heaven, shineth unto the other part under heaven ; so shall also the Son of man be in his
day." This language agrees with that used by
Christ concerning his second coming. Matt. xxiv,
26, 27; Mark xiii, 21, 23. And instead of Luke

xvii, forming an objection to the position we have taken, it shows that the kingdom is yet future.

But if we were to admit that the kingdom was spiritual, (mystical,) and that it was established in the days of Christ's first advent, we should find ourselves involved in a great difficulty on Dan. ii, which shows that the kingdom of the God of heaven is not set up till the Roman Empire is divided into ten parts; whereas in the days of Christ, and for 300 years after, no such ten parts existed. The Roman Empire was divided into ten parts between the years 356 A. D., and 483. Then the image could not be smitten on the feet prior to 483 A. D., therefore, the kingdom of the God of heaven, brought to view by Daniel, was not established in the days of Christ's first advent,

Were we to claim that the image was smitten in the days of Christ, and that since that time the kingdom has been gradually set up, we should find facts against us; for, if you call the gospel the kingdom, where has it had the power to break one toe of the image in pieces? Facts show that instead of the stone's smiting the image, the image has smitten the stone all the way through the present dispensation; and for proof of this, read the history of the persecutions that have befallen the gospel church by the hands of the Pagan and Papal powers; for which, see *Fox's Book of Martyrs*, and *Buck's Theological Dictionary*.

Again, we see by reading Matt. xxv, 31--34, something further concerning the time when the kingdom shall be given to the saints for a possession, as also the locality of that kingdom.

" When the Son of man shall come in his glory, and all the holy angels with him, then shall he sit upon the throne of his glory, and before him shall be gathered all nations; and he shall separate them one from another, as a shepherd divideth his sheep from the goats: and he shall set the sheep on his right hand, but the goats on his left. Then shall the King say unto them on his right hand, Come, ye blessed of my Father, inherit the kingdom prepared for you from the foundation of the world."

What kingdom was prepared from the foundation of the world? According to this text, it is the one the saints are to inherit. Are the saints at that time called to inherit heaven as a kingdom? If you say, yes, we would ask, Was the heaven which you suppose the saints are to inhabit, where God dwells, prepared at the foundation of the world? We can conceive of no kingdom that was prepared from the foundation of the world, but the earth itself. When God had created the earth, and beautified it, and pronounced it very good, he gave man dominion-over it. Gen. i, 26. As we are told, [Micah iv, 8,] this first dominion is to come to Christ, so the kingdom prepared *from* the foundation of the world, is the earth itself.

The above text also furnishes some evidence as to the time of the giving of the dominion and greatness of the kingdom under the whole heavens unto the people of the saints of the Most High. It is when the Son of man is seated on the throne of his glory, and all nations are gathered before him, and he makes a final separation, consigning one party to the flames and receiving the other to possess the kingdom. It has been argued, quite conclusively

4

too, that the wicked cannot be thus consigned to the flames till after their resurrection, which Rev. xx, locates at the end of the 1000 years, after Christ's second advent, as it also does their destruction. And, therefore, the time when the saints are called to possess this earth as a kingdom must be a thousand years after Christ's second advent, as it could not otherwise be after the resurrection of the wicked.

Certain it is, according to Peter's argument, that it is after the earth is made new that the saints are to receive it for an inheritance. "We look for new heavens and a new earth, wherein dwelleth righteousness." The earth is to become an abode for the righteous after it is purified by fire; and yet, after that purification, it will be the earth that it is now, in the same sense that this earth is the one that existed before the flood. This earth is composed of the same material that existed before the flood, and yet it is said, that "the world that then was, being overflowed with water, perished." And so of this earth, when it has been melted and undergone a change by the action of fire, it will become a new earth, in which the saints will dwell.

If this earth is not to become the abode of the saints until it is made new, we see it will have quite a bearing in the settlement of the question when the kingdom is established on earth, to learn, if possible, when the earth is made new. Peter says, [2 Pet. iii, 10.] The day of the Lord will come, *in* the which this earth is to be melted, and a new earth is to be brought in. This, of course, does not fix the definite point when this change shall take place, further than that it is said to be *in* that day.

The day of the Lord we understand commences
with events just prior to Christ's second coming,
and concludes after the wicked are destroyed for
ever out of the earth, which we see by Rev. xx, is in
the "little season" after the thousand years. So
this text would not fix the definite point for that
event, save that it shows that it will be *in* the day
of the Lord.

At what point in that day is the new earth
brought in? now becomes an important question.
Some have argued that it will be at the very commencement of that day; that at Christ's second advent the saints will be caught up to meet the Lord
in the air, and that they will then enter the New
Jerusalem while the wicked are being destroyed,
and the earth melted. Some have claimed that
there the Prophet's testimony applies: [Isa. xxvi,
20:] "Come, my people, enter thou into thy chambers, and shut thy doors about thee; hide thyself
as it were for a little moment until the indignation
be overpast." Although we agree with the position that this text is a call for God's people to hide
themselves while this earth is undergoing its purging by fire, yet from the testimony that immediately follows, we conclude it cannot apply till after the
thousand years. "For, behold, the Lord cometh
out of his place to punish the inhabitants of the
earth for their iniquity; the earth also shall dis·
close her blood, and shall no more cover her slain."
Here is a coming of the Lord out of his place,
and the special object of that coming is stated.
When he thus comes to punish them, the earth no
more covers her slain. So it must be that at that
point all the wicked are **resurrected**, which to our

mind is conclusive evidence that this text has a better application at the end of the thousand years.

What to us seems a serious difficulty, presents itself in the way of the view that the new earth is brought in at the beginning of the thousand years. It seems from Peter's testimony that when this purifying of the earth takes place, the works in it are destroyed. But is it consistent to suppose that after this earth has been cleansed one thousand years, and during that time been the place "wherein dwelleth righteousness," that all the wicked rebels that ever were upon it, shall be resurrected in one vast body out of the purified earth, and go up on its beautiful plains with Satan at their head, and that then fire and brimstone is rained from heaven upon those glorious fields of verdure to destroy the wicked?

By the above remarks, we do not dispute that the wicked will be raised at the end of the thousand years; that they will come round the New Jerusalem and be destroyed. And then we understand is the time when they shall "see Abraham, Isaac, and Jacob in the kingdom, and they themselves thrust out." The kingdom, we understand is first established in the city, and that finally when the earth is purified, the "dominion and greatness of the kingdom" will be "under the whole heavens." If the earth is made new, and the wicked are upon it when they see the kingdom, they would virtually be in the kingdom, and how could they then see "themselves thrust out?" Again, If the whole earth is made new and constitutes the kingdom when they behold it, where is their stand point from which they can behold, and be themselves out of the kingdom? But it is all plain with the view above suggested, that the kingdom is first established in the city, and after the wicked are cut off and the earth cleansed that the dominion is extended under the whole heaven.

It has been supposed by some that Christ's kingdom cannot be established at all, until he takes possession of the whole earth, destroys the wicked, and establishes a peaceful reign upon it; but we do not understand that that is necessary. When he establishes his kingdom, the heathen are given into his hands that he may "break them with a rod of iron, and dash them in pieces like a potter's vessel." The LORD says of Christ, [Ps. ii,] "Ask of me, and I shall give thee the heathen for thine inheritance, and the uttermost parts of the earth for thy possession." This we understand takes place when the testimony of Dan. vii, 13, 14, is fulfilled: "I saw in the night visions, and, behold, one like the Son of man came with the clouds of heaven, and came to the Ancient of days, and they brought him near before him. And there was given him dominion and glory, and a kingdom," &c. Some suppose this to refer to Christ's second coming. This cannot be, for when he comes the second time, he comes away from the Father; but this testimony speaks of a time when he is "brought near before him" to receive a kingdom. And in the parable of the nobleman going into a far country to receive a kingdom, we read: "When he was returned, *having received* the kingdom." So he receives the kingdom before he returns. But at this point we will notice

54 THE SAINTS' INHERITANCE.

THE THOUSAND YEARS OF REV. XX.

Perhaps a query has already been raised in the
minds of our readers concerning the thousand yea s'
reign of the saints, and the condition of the earth
during that thousand years. From the positions
taken in this work, that the saints will not inherit
the earth until it is made new, and that the earth
is not made new until the wicked are destroyed, it
would be justly inferred that the saints do not inherit the earth until after the thousand years. So it
is demanded here that something should be said concerning the position of the saints during the thous-
and years, also concerning the condition of the
earth.

Various opinions are extant concerning the one
thousand years, and it cannot be expected that in
this brief work we shall go into a detailed examination of all those views, but we wish to throw out
some ideas, which, if received, will in themselves
meet these various positions concerning the thousand
years.

Perhaps we are safe in making the assertion that
all are agreed that this thousand years when Satan
is bound, is at the end of six thousand years from
creation, (which are now nearly expired,*) for there

*According to Usher's Chronology, (that of our Bi-
bles,) the creation was 4004 years before the first advent
of Christ, which would make the world about 5863 years
old. But there is one place where Usher stands correct-
ed by the Apostle Paul. It is in the reign of the judges. All Chronologers have admitted this as the most
difficult period to compute. Usher has given the judges only three hundred years, but Paul says, [Acts xiii,
20.] "And after that he gave unto them judges about
the space of four hundred and fifty years, until Samuel

are so few exceptions that they are of no note. The great difference of opinion is in regard to the work of that period, rather than the period itself. One class claim that this thousand years is prior to Christ's second advent, during which all the world is to enjoy a peaceful reign, having been converted at the commencement of that period. But we consider that we have said sufficient in this work to refute the idea of the world's ever being converted, or of a millennium prior to the second advent of Christ.

Another class have taken the position that the thousand years' reign is on the earth, after the second advent of Christ, before the earth is renewed. This position to us seems the wildest of fancies, especially as the idea has been connected with it, that during that period probation is still to continue, and in that thousand years the saints will reign over, and teach mortal nations who are to increase during that period; and the Devil is to be let loose at the end of that period and deceive that company who have never known his wiles, (and even those holding these views cannot show that one of those among whom Satan is permitted to go, escapes his deceptions,) and those deceived are all devoured by fire from God.

Some of the principal reasons urged for this faith, we shall briefly notice.

First. Two texts are collated together and made to read as though they were one: "They lived and

the prophet." Paul does not say it was exactly that number of years, but *about*. This difference being added to Usher's Chronology, makes the world now about 6000 years old.

reigned with Christ a thousand years." Rev. xx, 4. And, " We *shall* reign on the earth." Chap. v, 10. Now we believe the testimony of both these texts, but they do not say that the saints will reign on earth a thousand years. They will reign on earth for ever and ever, but that will be in the "new earth wherein dwelleth righteousness," or wherein the righteous shall dwell. The text does not represent that Christ will reign on earth a thousand years; but "they shall reign *with Christ* a thousand years!"

Second. The claim is, if the saints *reign* a thousand years, they must have somebody to reign over, and so it is claimed that they reign over mortals. But if they cannot reign a thousand years unless they have mortals to reign over, who are on probation, how can they reign for ever and ever without the same?

Christ's promise to the twelve apostles was, " Ye also shall sit upon twelve thrones, *judging* the twelve tribes of the children of Israel." Matt. xix, 28. Then the saints are, at some point, to reign with Christ, and in that reign accomplish a work of judgment. This is to be " when the Son of man shall sit in the throne of his glory." Paul also inquires, [1 Cor. vi, 2, 3,] "Do ye not know that the saints shall judge the world? . . . know ye not that we shall judge angels? how much more things that pertain to this life?" This judgment is contrasted with judgment concerning things pertaining to this life, and therefore we understand it to refer to a future judgment. We read also in Ps. cxlix, 5, 9: "Let the saints be joyful in glory. . . . Let the high praises of God be in their mouth, and a two-edged sword in their hands, . . . to execute upon them the judgment written : this honor have all his saints." From the above texts we learn that there is a work to occupy the thousand years' reign, although there may be no mortal nations for saints to reign over during that period. The saints are to participate with Christ, in passing sentence on the wicked nations of earth.

When the saints sing, " We *shall* reign on the earth," they are already kings and priests, and are prostrating themselves before the throne in heaven. They sing of Christ, "Thou hast redeemed us to God by thy blood out of every tongue, and kindred, and people, and nation." Although this language quoted is the language of the four beasts and four and twenty elders, it is probably what all the saints will sing after their final deliverance. If this is the case, then the saints will, at some time, go to heaven, and thus prostrate themselves in adoration before the throne.

THE SAINTS WILL GO TO HEAVEN.

Those who claim that the thousand years' reign will be on earth, generally claim that the saints will never go to heaven; and therefore, if they reign a thousand years, it must be on earth. Our reply is, The word says, " They shall reign WITH CHRIST a thousand years;" and we shall proceed to show that at the commencement of the thousand years, at least, they are *with* Christ in heaven. There is no direct evidence to show that the thousand years' reign is upon earth, or that the saints will be on the earth again after their ascension, till the end of the thousand years; we have hence concluded that the thousand years' reign is in heaven.

But we will produce some additional evidence that the saints will go to heaven. Paul's testimony in 1 Thess. iv, is, "The Lord himself shall descend from heaven with a shout, with the voice of the archangel, and with the trump of God: and the dead in Christ shall rise first; then we which are alive and remain, shall be caught up together with them in the clouds, to meet the Lord in the air; and so shall we ever be with the Lord." But, says one, they immediately come down again, and possess the earth. Our reply is, That is all assumption; for there is no evidence to prove that they are on earth again till the end of the thousand years, when the wicked are said to "come around the camp of the saints and the beloved city." But there is evidence to show that after they are redeemed they go to heaven and sing the song of redemption. We read, [Rev. xv, 2, 3.] "And I saw as it were a sea of glass mingled with fire: and them that had gotten the victory over the beast, and over his image, and over his mark, and over the number of his name, stand on the sea of glass, having the harps of God. And they sing the song of Moses the servant of God, and the song of the Lamb." Here is a company that are to stand (after they are delivered) "*on the sea of glass.*" Where is the sea of glass? John tells us in Rev. v, 1, 6: "After this I looked, and, behold, a door was opened in heaven." We read of many things which he saw; but in verse 6 he says: "And before the throne there was a sea of glass like unto crystal." There can be no dispute as to the locality of the sea of glass. It is immediately before the throne

of God in heaven. Here then is direct evidence
that the saints will go to heaven, for they are to
sing the song of their deliverance on the sea of
glass, which we find is before the throne of God
in heaven.

Again, Christ's teaching to his diciples, as recorded in John xiii and xiv, is proof that the saints
will go to heaven at his second advent. In chap.
xiii, 33, we read; " Little children, yet a little while
I am with you. Ye shall seek me, and as I said
unto the Jews, whither I go, ye cannot come; so
now I say to you. Simon Peter said unto him,
[verse 36,] Lord, whither goest thou? Jesus answered him, Whither I go, thou canst not follow
me now; but thou shalt follow me afterwards."
Christ had told the Jews, [John vii, 33,] "I go
unto him that sent me." Then Christ's testimony
to Peter is: Thou canst not now follow me to heav-
en, or to him that sent me, but thou shalt follow
me to him that sent me after I have been there.
In the commencement of chap. xiv, Christ shows
them just how this promise to Peter shall be veri-.
fied: " Let not your heart be troubled; ye believe
in God, believe also in me. In my Father's house
are many mansions : if it were not so, I would have
told you. I go to prepare a place for you. And
if I go and prepare a place for you, I will come
again and receive you unto myself; that where I am,
there ye may be also." Here again is direct evidence
that the saints will go to heaven with Christ after
his second coming. All must admit that the first
verses of John xiv, are an explanation of what Christ
had told Peter; namely, Thou canst not follow me
now to him that sent me, for that testimony was

the very thing which had troubled the hearts of the disciples.

Inasmuch as there is no testimony to show that the saints do not go to heaven with Christ after his second advent, we claim that the opposite is fully sustained by the testimony we have noticed. The saints are to "reign *with* Christ a thousand years." We have found already that they commence that thousand years *before the throne* IN HEAVEN. Who will venture to claim that the thousand years' reign is on earth, with no evidence that there is a man on earth from the time the thousand years commence, till they end? But, says one, there are certain promises which have been made to certain nations, that have never been fulfilled; and they cannot be fulfilled in the new earth state. and so we have concluded they will be fulfilled during the thousand years, when the saints will reign over mortal nations, and those nations will be on probation, and many of them become converted. We have not space here to notice, one by one, those peculiar promises that are spoken of, but we shall object to the conclusion that has been drawn concerning those promises.

To claim that men can find pardon for their sins after the second advent of Christ, is to strike against the plainest declaration of holy writ. Says Christ. [Rev. xxii, 11,] "He that is unjust, let him be unjust still; and he which is filthy, let him be filthy still; and he that is righteous, let him be righteous still: and he that is holy, let him be holy still. And behold I come quickly." Here we learn that just previous to Christ's coming, the solemn decree goes forth, showing that each class must still occupy the position in which they then stand. But, says one, the class who are to have probation, are neither just nor unjust. We reply, There is no such class recognized in the word of God. Says Christ, "He that is not with me, is against me ; and he that gathereth not with me, scattereth abroad."

Concerning those promises before referred to, a portion of them have been fulfilled. Many of them are conditional ; for the conditions are distinctly expressed, and as the people failed to fulfill the conditions on their part, of course, the promise being conditional, becomes null and void. Of promises that have reference to national blessings, I see not how they could be otherwise than conditional. To claim that God will bless a nation irrespective of its character, is contrary to all his past dealings with his people. Although there may be instances where promises of national blessings are given, and no condition expressed, yet such condition is always to be understood. The Lord says, [Jer. xviii, 7–10,] "At what instant I shall speak concerning a nation, and concerning a kingdom, to pluck up, and to pull down, and to destroy it; if that nation, against whom I have pronounced, turn from their evil, I will repent of the evil that I thought to do unto them. And at what instant I shall speak concerning a nation, and concerning a kingdom, to build and to plant it; if it do evil in my sight, that it obey not my voice, then I will repent of the good, wherewith I said I would benefit them."

There is no principle recognized in the word of God, by which pardon can be obtained after the second advent of Christ. It cannot be effected by

the mediation of Christ; for that ends when he
lays aside his priestly garments and takes his position as a King. When Christ ceases his mediation,
he that is unrighteous must be so still. Mercy then
no longer pleads. The offering of beasts could be
of no avail, for Christ has for ever cut the wicked
off from having any interest in his blood; they
must remain filthy still. If they offer beasts, the
blood of beasts cannot take away sins. Because
there is no principle recognized for salvation ex-
cept the intercession of Jesus, we can see no
chance for salvation after that intercession ends; so
there can be no probation after his second advent.
It is argued that " Christ's kingdom is not a sky
kingdom; but the earth is the territory of the kingdom." And " if the kingdom is established at the
coming of Christ, it must be that the thousand
years' reign is on the earth." Now I shall not dis-
agree with the first position that the earth is to become finally the kingdom; for " the kingdom and
dominion, and the greatness of the kingdom under
the whole heavens," is to be given to the saints of
the Most High. It is the *new earth*, however, that
is to be the inheritance of the saints. As regards
the kingdom's being established at the coming of
Christ, we understand his kingdom does commence
when he puts on his kingly robes. The govern-
ment, or kingdom, we understand is fully organ-
ized in the city above, and when sinners are destroyed out of the earth and the earth made new,
the dominion and greatness of that kingdom will
be under the whole heavens. We are now led to
inquire into the

CONDITION OF THE EARTH DURING THE THOUSAND YEARS.

A query doubtless arises in the mind of the reader: If the reign of a thousand years is in heaven, and the kingdom is not established on earth till after that period, what is the condition of the earth during the thousand years? Whatever condition it is placed in at the commencement of that period, must be its condition to the close, unless we have evidence to the contrary. We read in Isa. xxiv, 1: " Behold, the Lord maketh the earth empty, and maketh it waste, and turneth it upside down, and scattereth abroad the inhabitants thereof." Verse 3. " The land shall be *utterly emptied*, and utterly spoiled: for the Lord hath spoken this word." Verses 5, 6. " The earth also is defiled under the inhabitants thereof: because they have transgressed the laws, changed the ordinance, broken the everlasting covenant. Therefore hath the curse devoured the earth, and they that dwell therein are desolate : therefore the inhabitants of the earth are burned, and few men left."

But, says one, it cannot be that this text proves the entire desolation of the earth; for there are " few men left." It does not say there are a few men left on the earth, but the testimony is that the " Lord maketh the earth EMPTY." " The land shall be *utterly emptied*," &c. Then these few men left, are not on earth. We suppose those who are left are the saints, who, we have already shown, will go to heaven with Jesus after his second advent.

Jeremiah describes [Jer. iv, 23--27] the state of things after the earth is turned upside down: " I beheld the earth, and lo, it was without form and void ; and the heavens, and they had no light. I beheld the mountains, and, lo, they trembled, and all the hills moved lightly. I beheld, and, lo, there was *no man,* and all *the birds of the heavens were fled.* I beheld, and, lo, the fruitful place was a wilderness, and all the cities thereof were broken down at the presence of the Lord, and by his fierce anger. For thus hath the Lord said, *The* WHOLE LAND *shall* BE DESOLATE; yet will I not make a full end." The Lord will not make a full end, for the good reason that the earth is to be restored, and then it will be given to man as his inheritance. The quotation above shows as desolate a condition of the earth, as when God first spoke it into existence. This desolation is in the day of the Lord, and as there is no proof that there is a man on earth again till the end of the thousand years, our position is that it is utterly emptied during that period.

We read in Zeph. i, 2, 3 : " I will *utterly consume all things* from off the land, saith the Lord. I will consume man and beast; I will consume the fowls of the heaven, and the fishes of the sea, and the stumbling-blocks with the wicked ; and I will *cut off man from off the land,* saith the Lord." By reading verse 7, we learn when this is to be. " Hold thy peace at the presence of the Lord God : for *the day of the Lord is at hand :* for the Lord hath prepared a sacrifice, he hath bid his guests." In Rev. xix, 17 we read of " an angel standing in the sun ; and he cried with a loud voice, saying to all the fowls that fly in the midst of heaven, Come, and gather yourselves to the supper of the great

God." This is probably the sacrifice and guests to which the prophet refers.

In Isa. xiii, 9, we read: "Behold the day of the Lord cometh, cruel both with wrath and fierce anger, TO LAY THE LAND DESOLATE: and he shall destroy the sinners thereof out of it." The day of the Lord will desolate the land: so there are no mortal nations for the saints to reign over. The wicked dead have no resurrection till the end of the thousand years; and as the reign of the saints is *with Christ*, the earth must be desolate during the thousand years.

At the end of that period, as recorded by Zechariah, [chap. xiv,] Christ's feet will stand on the mount of Olives, and the mount of Olives will cleave half toward one sea, and half toward the other, and there will be formed a mighty plain. Upon that plain we understand that the city, New Jerusalem, comes down. The wicked are then resurrected, [Rev. xx,] Satan goes out to deceive them, they gather around the camp of the saints, and the beloved city, and fire comes down from God out of heaven and devours them. That fire which burns up the wicked, burns up the works of the Devil which are in the earth. By that fire the mountains are melted and run down like wax, and thus the deep caverns of earth are filled. The curse is forever swept from the earth, and when the fires of that day have subsided, the earth will stand forth in its restored state, beautiful and glorious, and will become the everlasting abode of the saints of God —the new earth wherein dwelleth righteousness, which Peter says we look for according to God's

5

promise, In noticing this promise we shall endeav-
or to give a

DESCRIPTION OF THE KINGDOM.

Human language is hardly adequate for the task,
to set forth the glories of the better land; for, as
Paul says, " Eye hath not seen, nor ear heard, neither
have entered into the heart of man the things which
God hath prepared for them that love him; but
God hath revealed them unto us by his Spirit."
While here, as he says, " we see through a glass
darkly, but then face to face." As a person looking through a darkened glass at the broad sun may
get a correct outline of its disc, and yet its resplen-
dent glory is hid, so we, by giving heed to those
things which God has " revealed by his Spirit," may
get an outline of that glorious kingdom, and yet
not comprehend the glory which can be better felt
than told.

Peter says, according to God's promise " we look
for new heavens and a new earth." This promise
is recorded in Isa. lxv. Peter, as we have before
shown, reasons from this promise that the present
heavens and earth are to be melted, and the works
therein (dross) to be burned up. David is probably speaking of the same [Ps. cii, 26] when he says:
"Yea, all of them shall wax old like a garment;
as a vesture shalt thou *change* them, and they shall
be *changed*."

Peter, according to his testimony recorded in
Acts iii, 21, looks forward to the time when Christ
shall come to accomplish this work, and calls it
" The times of restitution." John, while receiving

his testimony on the isle of Patmos, heard a voice from Him which sat upon the throne, which said, "Behold I make all things *new;*" (not all new things.) David doubtless had his mind on the same point when he penned the testimony of Ps. civ, 30, where he speaks of the Lord's "*renewing* the face of the earth."

But we will pass these points to notice Isaiah's testimony. He says, "For behold I create new heavens and a new earth: and the former shall not be remembered, nor come into mind." Isa. lxv, 17. Here is the very promise Peter calls our attention to. "And I will rejoice in Jerusalem, and joy in my people: and the voice of weeping shall no more be heard in her, nor the voice of crying." Verse 19. This agrees with John's view of the matter, recorded in Rev. xxi, 4. "God shall wipe away all tears from their eyes." Some read this as though it meant, literally, as expressed by the poet,

"His own soft hand shall wipe the tears
From every weeping eye,"

and the people still be left with sadness in their hearts. Not so: "What God doeth, he doeth it forever." How does the Lord wipe away tears? We answer, By removing forever from among his people every cause of grief. When Christ tells us [Rev. xxi, 4] that God shall wipe away all tears, he assigns the reason, "And there shall be no more death, neither shall there be any more pain." Yes,

"*Pains* and *groans* and *griefs* and *fears,*
And *death* itself shall die."

Verse 20. "There shall be no more thence an infant of days, nor an old man that hath not filled his days: for the child shall die an hundred years old; but the sinner being an hundred years old shall be accursed." There have, in times past, been many speculative notions advanced on the above text, in order to produce a harmony between it and other testimonies which speak of the same time, (the new-earth state,) as one in which there is to be *no* death. The first clause of the above verse, shows that there will "be no more *thence*," from the time the new-earth state is brought in, "an infant of days," (a short-lived child,) "or an old man who hath not filled his days," (premature old age.) All will eternally glow with the vigor of youth. The latter clause of the verse speaks of death, and cannot therefore apply to the new earth, for of the new earth state, John says: "There shall be no more death." If we abide by the rendering of king James' version, it must apply to what transpires just as that state is ushered in. The sinner, although he be an hundred years old, is accursed: Not permitted to enter the land, and dies *a child*, compared to the endless life those are to enjoy who live in the new earth state.

Some writers have adopted on this text, the reading given by Paganini, which is, "There shall be no more carried out thence to burial, an infant of days, or a youth, or an old man who hath not filled his days; for the man of a hundred years shall be as a youth." This rendering of the above text, certainly produces a harmony, and must be the idea designed to be conveyed, if the 20th verse is to be applied after the new-earth state is brought in.

"And they shall build houses, and inhabit them; and they shall plant vineyards and eat the fruit of them. They shall not build, and another inhabit; they shall rot plant and another eat." Verses 21, 22. Some object, and say, can it be that the saints will build and plant in the new earth? It says so. Where will you apply the testimony, if you attempt to refer it to the present state? Where is the man of whom it can be said that he shall not build, and another inhabit. Men here spend their whole lives, fitting up an inheritance to their taste, and just as they pronounce it fitted to their mind. they find themselves old men, die, and leave it to others.

"For as the days of *a tree* are the days of my people ; and mine elect shall long enjoy the work of their hands." Verse 22. As the days of what tree? I reply the tree of life;* and if that be the tree referred to, then they will live forever; for God drove Adam out of the garden, lest he should put forth his hand and " eat of the tree of life and live forever." See Gen. iii. This reminds me of another testimony, in which the Lord says: " With long life will I satisfy him and show him my salvation." Ps. xci,16. A query arises here, namely : How long a life would it require to satisfy a man? If a man's body was racked with disease, and his life made bitter by disappointment and sorrow, he might perhaps come to a point where he could say, I have lived long enough, I want to die; but if he was surrounded with every thing that tended to his comfort and happiness, in a state where there was no death, no sorrow, no pain, no tears, would he be satisfied with anything short of eternal life? I think not.

Verses 23,24, show God's willingness to answer
*So the Septuagint.

and do for his people, and that in that time the labor of their hands shall prosper and not be brought forth for trouble. Verse 25. "The wolf and the lamb shall feed together, and the lion shall eat straw like the bullock, and dust shall be the serpent's meat." This can only apply in a state where the ferocious dispositions of the wolf and lion have been changed. But, says one, can the above apply in the kingdom of God? Are the saints to eat there? Yes. Christ ate after his resurrection, [Luke xxiv, 42,43.] If Christ ate why may not the saints? They are to be like him. See 1 John iii, 1, 2; Phil. iii, 21. Angels eat.

They appeared to Lot, and ate of the food he prepared. Gen. xix,3. David says of the Israelites: "Man did eat angels' food." Ps. lxxviii,25. The resurrected saints are to be as the angels. Luke xx,36. But Christ has declared that they will eat in the kingdom: "And I appoint unto you a kingdom, as my Father hath appointed unto me; that ye may *eat* and *drink* at my table in my kingdom, and sit on thrones, judging the twelve tribes of Israel." Luke xxii,29,30. Again Christ says: "Blessed are those servants, whom the Lord when he cometh shall find watching; verily I say unto you, that he shall gird himself, and make them to sit down to meat, and will come forth and serve them." Luke xii, 37.

"But," you say, "I did not think there were to be beasts in the kingdom of God." If the kingdom of God is to be a restitution to the primeval state, there will be beasts there. In Eden the Lord gave man "dominion over the fish of the sea, and over the fowl of the air, and over the cattle, and over all the earth, and over every creeping thing that creepeth on the earth." Gen. i,26. And Micah testifies concerning Christ, [Chap. iv,8.] "And thou, O tower of the flock, the stronghold of the daughter of Zion, unto thee shall it come, even the first dominion." If the first dominion comes to Christ, then he will have dominion over beasts as well as the earth and man. That the dominion which is to be given to Christ, is the dominion of the earth, is confirmed by David's testimony, [Ps. lxxii,8:] "He shall have *dominion* also from sea to sea, and *from the river unto the ends of the earth.*" David's testimony also shows that there will be beasts in the " renewed" state. In Ps. civ, 29,30, after speaking of beasts, &c., he says: " Thou hidest thy face, they are troubled; thou takest away their breath, they die and return to their dust. Thou sendest forth thy spirit, they are created; and thou *renewest* the face of the earth."

We wish now to look at a testimony in Isaiah xi. By reading from the 1st to the 5th verse, you will see that this testimony concerning the " Rod out of the stem of Jesse," cannot refer to any earthly monarch; for they have no way of judging, but " after the sight of the eyes," nor to reprove but "after the hearing of the ears." We also learn that this personage is the one who is to slay the wicked with his breath, and also, that what follows from the 6th to the 9th verse, is after he has thus slain the wicked. This, then, refers to Christ's kingdom. Let us read a description of it: " The wolf also shall dwell with the lamb, and the leopard shall lie down with the kid; and the calf and the young lion and the fatling together; and a little child shall lead them. And the cow and the bear shall feed; their young ones shall lie down together; and the lion shall eat straw like the ox. And the sucking child shall play on the hole of the asp, and the weaned child shall put his hand on the cockatrice's, (margin adder's) den." Here again we have a description of a state, when the evil dispositions of the beasts are taken away, and when the manner of their living even is changed. And the 9th verse shows that " They shall not hurt nor destroy in all my holy mountain; for the earth shall be full of the knowledge of the Lord, as the waters cover the sea."— This we have already shown cannot be, till after Christ comes and subdues all his foes.

"Then, bears and wolves no longer wild,
    Obey the leading of a child ;
The lions with the oxen eat,
    And dust shall be the serpent's meat."

Those who deny the application of the above text, and Isaiah lxv, to a future state, claim that it is fulfilled here. Their claim is, that " this testimony is mystical, and has a hidden meaning. That these beasts, the wolf, lion, kid, and lamb, are used to represent men with different dispositions, whose hearts are softened and subdued by the ameliorating influence of the gospel." " The text," they say, " is fulfilled, when a man with a wolfish or lion-like disposition, is converted and brought into the fold of Christ, and with the lambs (christians) feeds on the heavenly manna." We object to this application for two reasons: First, when a man with a wolfish or lion-like disposition is converted, he is no longer a wolf or lion, but a lamb; and so in the sequel, those who make the above application of the text, will simply have two lambs feeding together, instead of a lion and a lamb. So to make the text bear the above application which they desire, it will be necessary for them to claim that men with un-changed hearts, and lives, are brought into the church, and feed on the heavenly manna.

Our second objection is, it is positively stated, (Isaiah lxv, 17-25,) that there shall be such a state of things in the new earth.

Thus we see, allowing these testimonies a literal application, a glorious scene is portrayed to our mind when the curse is removed, and the "fear of man" (Gen. ix, 2,) is so far taken away that the beasts are again in perfect subjection to him, as in the beginning, (Gen. i, 26,) even to that extent that "the little child shall lead" the fierce lion, "the king of the forest."

Again, Isaiah describes the saints' inheritance in chapter xxxv,1-7: "The wilderness and the solitary place shall be glad for them; and the desert shall rejoice and blossom as the rose." On the Sahara, and great desert of Arabia, the weary traveler now plods his way, scorched with the burning rays of the sun, finding no cooling shade beneath which to rest his aching limbs, but, faint with thirst, he lays himself down to die. No merry songsters beguile his sufferings and as his voice grows husky and still, nothing meets his vision but a vast plain of burning sand: not one beautiful flower to change the sad monotony of the desert; and in the distance, the driving Simoon threatening to bury him in its columns of sand. How changed the scene when the "restitution" work shall have been accomplished. "The desert shall blossom as

the rose." Yes, and it shall " rejoice even with joy
and singing." When it is clothed with green foliage
and decked with blossoms abundant, the merry
songsters will chirp from bough to bough, and
warble forth their songs of praise to the Most
High.

Verse 2. "It shall blossom abundantly and rejoice even with joy and singing; the glory of Lebanon, (the forest of Lebanon is described as the
most beautiful in appearance of any in the eastern
world) shall be given to it, the excellency of Car-
mel and Sharon." The valley of Sharon was an-
ciently decorated with the most beautiful flowers
of every description. In view of this glorious clothing which is to be given to the desert, the prophet
says, [verses 3, 4,] " Strengthen ye the weak hands,
and confirm the feeble knees. Say to them that
are of a fearful heart, *Be strong*, *fear not;* behold
your God will come with vengeance, even God with
a recompense ; he will come and save you."

Who would not feel strengthened with a hope
of such a glorious inheritance as this, constantly before him? These promises have been given, not
only that we might know what is coming, but to
impart strength to us who are heirs of promise.—
Reader, are you a believer in these glorious promises ?
We would say to you, when your heart gets fearful
amid the trials and conflicts of the way, look at
these hope-inspiring records respecting the future,
and " *be strong;*" for in Jesus' name, we are able
to go up and possess the goodly land. Thus Paul
could say : Our " *light affliction.*" " While we look
not at the things which are seen, *(the affliction)* but
at the things which are not seen; for the things

which are seen are temporal; but the things which are not seen, are eternal." 2 Cor. iv, 17, 18.

Isaiah continues in verses, 5, 6: "Then the eyes of the blind shall be opened, and the ears of the deaf shall be unstopped. Then shall the lame man leap as an hart, and the tongue of the dumb shall sing; for in the wilderness shall waters break out, and streams in the desert." As an aid to an understanding of the rejoicing of those who in that glorious state have been made free from all their infirmities, our mind turns to a case of healing, that was performed in the days of the Apostles, as recorded in Acts iii. A man who had been lame from his birth, who was daily laid at the beautiful gate of the temple, to ask alms, saw Peter and John about to go into the temple, and asked an alms.— He expected no relief from his infirmity, but asked a little pittance to enable him to protract his miserable existence here. When Peter said to him "Look on us," his expectation was raised that they would give him a portion of money; but when Peter said, "Silver and gold have I none," his hopes in that direction were blasted, and how unexpected must the next sentence have fallen on his ears:— "Such as I have give I thee: In the name of Jesus Christ of Nazareth, *rise up and walk!* And he took him by the right hand and lifted him up; and immediately his feet and ancle-bones received strength." What a thrill of joy must have filled his heart at this unexpected healing of his infirmities. He "entered with them into the temple, walking and *leaping* and praising God." If this temporary relief would cause the poor cripple to *leap* for joy, what must be the feelings of those in the resurrection morn, who, all their lives have been bowed down with lameness and the infirmities of the flesh, when they find not only their feet and ancle-bones made straight, but their whole being glowing with the vigor and energy of eternal youth! " Then shall the lame man *leap* as an hart." They will go like the deer bounding through the forest, as they shout forth their praises to the Most High. Like David of old, they will dance " before the Lord with all their might."

Isaiah speaks again of this glorious state, chap. li, 3. "For the Lord shall comfort Zion; he will comfort all her waste places; and he will make her wilderness like Eden, and her desert like the garden of the Lord." In the garden of the Lord, planted eastward, in Eden, there was " every tree that was pleasant to the sight, and good for food." In the restitution, this will be the condition of the whole earth. As is stated in Isa. lv, 13, " Instead of the thorn, shall come up the fir tree, and instead of the briar, shall come up the myrtle tree." Thorns are a part of the curse that was put upon the earth.— Gen. iii, 18. But these are to be removed. In that glorious state God's people can " dwell safely in the wilderness, and sleep in the woods. . . . And the tree of the field shall yield her fruit, and the earth shall yield her increase, and they shall be safe in their land, and shall know that I am the Lord, when I have broken the bands of their yoke, and delivered them out of the hand of those that served themselves of them. And they shall no more be a prey to the heathen, neither shall the beasts of the land devour them: but they shall dwell safely, and none shall make them afraid." Ezek. xxxiv, 25, 27, 28.

And this is to be (verse 23,) when there is " set up
one shepherd over them," and when Christ, who is
here called by the Lord, " my servant David" "shall
be their shepherd," and " shall be a prince among
them."

We shall now examine John's testimony in Rev.
xxi, xxii, concerning the new-earth state: " And I
saw a new heaven and a new earth; for the first
heaven and the first earth were passed away." We
do not understand from this, that there is to be a
passing away of the matter of which the first heaven
and earth are composed. Peter has shown, as we
have already examined in the former part of this
book, that the new heavens and new earth is to be
brought in by the melting of the elements of the
present heavens and earth, and the burning up of
the works in the earth.

" And I, John, saw the holy city, New Jerusalem,
coming down from God, out of heaven, prepared as
a bride adorned for her husband. And I heard a
great voice out of heaven saying, behold, the tabernacle of God is with men, and he will dwell with
them, and they shall be his people, and God himself
shall be with them, and be their God. And God
shall wipe away all tears from their eyes; and there
shall be no more death, neither sorrow nor crying,
neither shall there be any more pain ; for the former things are passed away." Not only will these
not exist, but, as we have already seen, the opposite
will exist: life, joy, rejoicing, and eternal pleasures.
What a contrast with the present state of affliction,
weeping and death. No raging epidemic there,
sweeping its thousands into an untimely grave, and
in a moment filling joyous hearts with the keenest

anguish; no miasma or destructive thunderbolts; no funeral knell; no pall; no bier; no death-dirge will there be sung; no grave-yards ever greet our sight, and sadden our hearts with the thoughts of mortality; the grave-digger's spade will find no labor there ; no soothing cordial will be needed to still the aching limbs and weary head ; but immortality and the tree of life will forever accomplish the work, and free the saints from all liabilities to pain or suffering, Yes, "And the inhabitants will not say, I am sick." Isa. xxxiii, 24.

"*Death* will be banished, his scepter be gone."

Says JOHN WESLEY : ''We may more easily conceive the changes which will be wrought in the lower heaven, in the region of the air. It will be no more torn by hurricanes, or agitated by furious storms, or destructive tempests. Pernicious or terrifying meteors will have no place therein. We shall have no more occasion to say,

'There like a trumpet, loud and strong,
    Thy thunder shakes our coast;
While the red lightnings wave along,
    The banners of the host!'

"No ! all will then be light, fair and serene ; a lively picture of eternal day.

"And what will the general produce of the earth be ? Not thorns, briers and thistles; not any useless or fetid weed; not any poisonous, hurtful or unpleasant plant; but every one that can be conducive, in any wise, either to our use or pleasure. We shall no more regret the loss of the terrestrial paradise, or sigh at the well-devised description of our great poet :

' Then shall this mount
Of paradise by might of waves be moved
Out of its place, pushed by the horned flood,
With all its verdure spoiled, and trees adrift,
Down the great river to the opening gulf,
And there take root an island salt and bare.'

"For all the earth shall be a more beautiful paradise than Adam ever saw."*

Verses 9–16. " And there came unto me one of the seven angels which had the seven vials full of the seven last plagues, and talked with me, saying, Come hither, I will shew thee the bride, the Lamb's wife. And he carried me away in the Spirit to a great and high mountain, and shewed me that great city, the holy Jerusalem, descending out of heaven from God : having the glory of God: and her light was like unto a stone, most precious, even like a jasper stone clear as crystal; and had a wall great and high, and had twelve gates, and at the gates twelve angels, and names written thereon, which are the names of the twelve tribes of the children of Israel; on the east three gates; on the north three gates; on the south three gates; and on the west three gates. And the wall of the city had twelve foundations, and in them the names of the twelve apostles of the Lamb. And he that talked with me had a golden reed to measure the city, and the gates thereof, and the wall thereof. And the city lieth four square, and the length is as large as the breadth; and he measured the city with the reed, twelve thousand furlongs. The length and the breadth and the height of it are equal."

We understand that this measure of the city is its entire circumference; for the announcement is

*Sermon lxix. " Behold I make all things new."

made as soon as this measure is taken, that all sides are alike; length, breadth and height. The ancient custom of measuring cities was to begin at the corner and go entirely around, and not simply to measure one side. The measure of the city was twelve thousand furlongs. At eight furlongs to the mile, it would be fifteen hundred miles. This being the entire circumference of the city, one fourth of it would give us the length of eitner side: three hundred and seventy-five miles. Truly this is a *great* city. This is indeed the city that Abraham looked for, " which hath foundations, whose builder and maker is God." Heb. xi. This is the Jerusalem which Paul says " is above," and " is free, which is the mother of us all." It is the Father's house, in which Christ said " there are many mansions." It is the place he was going to prepare for his saints prior to his coming again to receive them to himself. John xiv, 1–3.

Verse 17. "And he measured the wall thereof, an hundred and forty and four cubits, according to the measure of a man, that is, of the angel." This we suppose to refer to the height of the wall, for he has already given us the length and the breadth. Eighteen inches to the cubit would give the height of the wall at two hundred and sixteen feet.

Verse 18. "And the building of the wall of it was of jasper; and the city was pure gold like unto clear glass." JASPER: "A precious stone of various colors, as purple, cerulean, green, &c." *Greenfield.* "Mostly green." *Robinson.* "Of a beautiful bright green color, sometimes clouded with white, and spotted with red or yellow." *Clarke.*

Verses 19, 20. And the *foundations* of the wall of

the city were garnished with all manner of precious stones. The first foundation was "*jasper;* the second, *sapphire;* the third, a *chalcedony;* the fourth, an *emerald;* the fifth, *sardonyx;* the sixth, *sardius;* the seventh, *chrysolite;* the eighth, *beryl;* the ninth, a *topaz;* the tenth, *chrysoprasus;* the eleventh, a *jacinth;* the twelfth, an *amethyst.*" These twelve stones are the *foundation* of the wall, but the wall is of jasper, which we have already described.

SAPPHIRE. "A precious stone of a blue color in various shades." *Greenfield, Robinson.* "A bright gem, properly of pure blue." *Cobbin.* "Perfectly transparent." *Clarke.* "Of a beautiful azure or sky-blue color, almost as transparent and glittering as a diamond." *Stuart.*

CHALCEDONY. "The name of a gem generally of a whitish, bluish, or smoky-green color, susceptible of a high and beautiful polish." *Geeenfield.* Some Greek MSS. read carbuncle, instead of chalcedony. *Carbuncle* "is a very elegant gem of a deep red color, with an admixture of scarlet. From its bright, lively color, it had the name, *carbunculus,* which signifies a little coal; because when held before the sun it appears like a bright burning charcoal." *Clarke.*

EMERALD, "is one of the most beautiful of all the gems, and is a bright green color, without any other mixture." *Clarke.*

SARDONYX. "A precious stone exhibiting a milk-white variety of the chalcedony, intermingled with shades or stripes of sardian or carnelian" (flesh color). *Robinson.*

SARDIUS. " A precious stone of blood-red, and sometimes flesh color." *Greenfield.*

" CHRYSOLYTE is of a beautiful yellow color, and is so called by the ancients from its looking like a golden stone." *Cobbin.*

BERYL, " is of a blueish green, and very brilliant." *Cobbin.*

" TOPAZ of the present day seems to be reckoned as yellow, but that of the ancients appears to have been green." *Stuart.*

CHRYSOPRASUS. "Its color is commonly apple-green, and often extremely beautiful." *Cleveland.*

JACINTH. " A precious stone of a dead red, with a mixture of yellow. It is the same as the hyacenet, or cinnamon stone." *Clarke.*

AMETHYST, " is a pure rock-crystal, of a purplish-violet color, and of great brilliancy." *Chambers.*

Stuart says of these precious stones : " There is classification therefore in the arrangement; a mixture not dissimilar to the rainbow, with the exception that it is more complex." And this forms the *foundation* of the *wall* of the city. That wall is itself bright green, spotted with red and yellow. In addition to this, it is transparent, so it will admit the rays of different colors to pass through it which emanate from the stones that form its foundation, (for many of these stones emit light of themselves.) Here is a scene of beauty, indeed; but when we contemplate still further, in addition to this, that the glory of God, which far outshines the sun, will cause those precious stones to sparkle and glisten, we have a wall of such splendor as is far beyond the conception of mortals.

Verse 21. "And the twelve gates were twelve pearls: every several gate was of one pearl. And the street of the city was pure gold, as it were transparent glass." Here is gold that is worth striving for. It is imperishable. One ounce of it would be worth more to you, dear reader, than all the gold of California. I would give more for a surety of enough of that gold to set my feet upon, than for all the treasures of earth. He that secures a standing-place on those streets will be safe.

Verse 23. "The city had no need of the sun, neither of the moon, to shine in it: for the glory of God did lighten it, and the Lamb is the light thereof." The glory of God will so far outshine the sun, that its rays will give no light in the city. This is not simply the sun as it now shines, but it is when as the Prophet says, "The light of the moon shall be as the light of the sun, and the light of the sun shall be seven fold." Isa. xxx, 26. Again, speaking of this same time [chap. xxiv, 23] he says: "Then the moon shall be confounded, and the sun ashamed, when the Lord of hosts shall reign in mount Zion, and in Jerusalem, and before his ancients gloriously." This refulgent light, shining on those most precious stones, will cause them to sparkle and glow, and shine forth such as by human sight hath never yet been seen.

Verse 24. "And the nations of them which are saved shall walk in the light of it; and the kings of the earth do bring their glory and honor into it." This it seems is to be the great metropolis, or capital of the new earth kingdom, into which all the nations of them that are saved shall come to offer their tribute of praise.

In chap. xxii, we have a description of the river of life "clear as crystal, proceeding out of the throne of God and the Lamb. In the midst of the street of it, and on either side of the river, was there the tree of life which bare twelve manner of fruits, and yielded her fruit every month: and the leaves of the tree were for the healing of the nations." Every month the tree will yield a fruit, and as God's saints, " from one new moon to another, and from one Sabbath to another come to worship before" the Lord, [Isa. lxvi, 23,] they may obtain of the fruits of the tree of life. Those who obey God's commandments, as we learn in chap. xxii, 14, are to have a right to the tree of life, and enter in through the gates into the city, and participate in this glorious rest.

Thus we have briefly investigated some of the many testimonies which speak of the glorious inheritance of the saints. The meek shall inherit the earth, as Christ has promised; but not till sin and the curse are removed. But says the objector, Christ said, "Great is your reward *in heaven.*" True, there is a rich reward reserved for us. We are to reign with Christ in heaven 1000 years, but that city with all its dazzling glory, as we have just seen from Rev. xxi, is to come down and be the capital of the earth restored. But, it is still urged, Paul said "we have a building of God, an house not made with hands, *eternal*, in the heavens." True, the building is *eternal*; but he does not say it will eternally remain there. God's word shows that it will come down and be the tabernacle of God, when he dwells with men.

CONCLUSION.

Dear reader, is not the inheritance God has promised good enough, especially when we consider that man, the participant of these glories, is to be clothed with immortality? " Flesh and blood cannot inherit the kingdom of God." But " when this corruptible shall have put on incorruption, and this mortal shall have put on immortality, then will God's saints be qualified to possess an immortal inheritance. Man will stand forth perfected, beauteous in form, free from pain, the stain of sin all washed away from his heart, and his lips shouting forth the praises of Him who has thus wrought for him. Methinks your better feelings say, It is glorious. Yes, and the best of all is, that state will *never* end. The countless ages of eternity will roll on, and

" When we've been there ten thousand years,
  Bright shining as the sun,
We've no less days to sing God's praise,
  Than when we first begun."

Dear reader, do you not feel a longing desire in your heart to be a partaker of the saints' inheritance? Don't you want to go to glory, and dwell with the angels, hear their rapturous songs, and sing with them? The Spirit calls you, there is yet room. The heavenly city, with all its charms, welcomes you to come. The way is easy, if you seek it through Christ.

First. " Break off from your sins by righteousness, and turn away from your transgressions by obedi-

ence to God." Have you no hope in Christ? speedily
obtain one. "If we confess and forsake our sins,
he is just and true to forgive us our sins, and cleanse
us from all unrighteousness." In the very day you
seek him with all the heart he will be found of you.
  Second. We must comply with the conditions
on which the promise was made. Christ says, "Blessed
are they that do His (the Father's) commandments
(the condition of the inheritance given to Abraham,) that they may have right to the tree of life,
and may enter in through the gates into the city."
Rev. xxii, 14. Then leave the trifles of earth.
Come away. Why will you linger and die? While
mercy lingers, why will you dally with the vanities
of earth, and neglect the preparation for that rich
inheritance which you may obtain?
  Are you a christian, striving to obtain a rich reward with the faithful? Take courage, the kingdom will be cheap enough, though you may wade
through seas of blood to obtain it. Contrast all
your afflictions here with that "far more exceeding
and eternal weight of glory" at the end of the race.
Cease your murmurings, heaven is cheap enough.
Remember, your trials here are only workmen sent
to polish you, and fit you for your heavenly inheritance.

  "Why should I murmur or repine at hardship, grief or
      loss?
  They only will the gold refine, and purge away the
      dross."

  God is displeased with murmuring christians.
Look how he recompensed those who murmured in
the wilderness. Paul has told us, "Neither murmur ye, as some of them also murmured." Be as

consistent in the heavenly way, as you are with
temporal matters. Let the object of your pursuit
spur you forward, and instead of murmuring at your
lot, let your actions tell to all that you consider that
object of greater value than worldly ease or pleasure.
If some lord of earth should come to your town and
advertise, saying, " Ho ! every one that is in my
hearing ! Any man who will labor for me carrying
wheat, shall receive a bushel of gold for every two
bushels of wheat he will carry a mile," what a rush
of people you would behold flocking to the scene of
action, each anxious to get a burden to carry. Behold them loading themselves to the ground almost,
with their heavy burdens. Why, the more load I
take the more gold I shall get, and you know I
can't go but once. See them trying their loads,
and concluding they " can carry a little more." On
they go. Down goes one. " Well," says another, "got
too much load ?" "Oh, no, I'll get along." Not
a word of complaining among that company. The
gold spurs them forward. Have you ever murmured ? Stop and think. An "*eternal weight of glory*" is to be worked out by this suffering. What?
Why, your "light affliction which is but for a *moment*, is working out for you an ETERNAL *weight* of
glory." The more afflictions the *heavier* the glory.
Well, I can carry a little more; for I have only to
carry it a *moment*, (compared with eternity,) and
Jesus says his grace is sufficient.

" The road may be rough, but it cannot be long,
I'll smoothe it with *hope*, and I'll cheer it with song."

Are you a minister of Christ, striving to lead the
flock in the way of God's truth, and win souls to

Christ? *Toil on.* "Thou shalt be recompensed at the resurrection of the just." He who has said, "Feed the flock of God," has also said, "When the chief Shepherd shall appear, ye shall receive a crown of glory that fadeth not away." Think often of the inheritance. No aching head, no hearts saddened there by opposition of men to God's truth. No fevered lungs worn with incessant labor; but there those who have turned many to righteousness "shall shine as the stars forever and ever." Toil on! and may we meet as fellow-laborers on mount Zion with the Lamb. Amen.

We'd love to have you download our catalog of titles we publish or even hear your thoughts, reactions, or criticism about this or any other book we publish at:

www.TEACHServices.com
or
info@TEACHServices.com

Or call us at:

518/358-3494

.

www.ingramcontent.com/pod-product-compliance
Lightning Source LLC
Chambersburg PA
CBHW060441090426
42733CB00011B/2352